Math

1

Grade 1

A Strange Fish

▶ Connect the dots. Start with **1**.

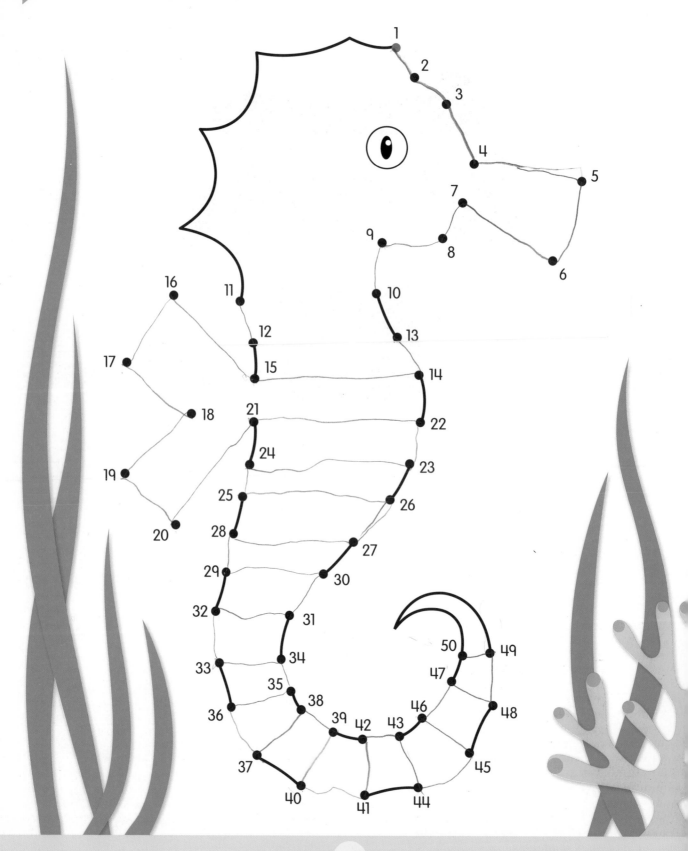

EMC 4175 • © Evan-Moor Corp.

Greater Than, Less Than

Write < or > in the circle.

8 is **greater than** 7	7 is **less than** 8
8 > 7	7 < 8

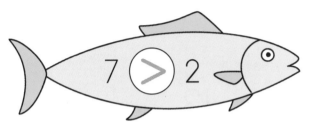

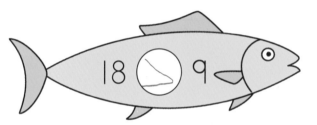

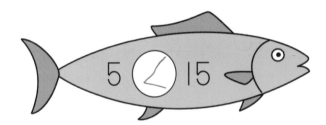

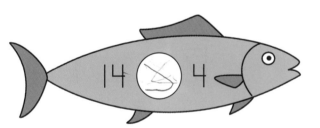

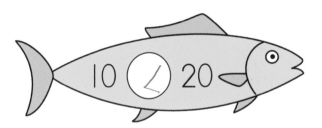

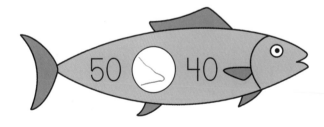

What's Missing?

▶ Write the missing numbers.

after	before	in between
21 _22_	_36_ 37	9 _10_ 11
39 _40_	_49_ 50	13 _14_ 15
45 _46_	_15_ 16	48 _49_ 50
17 _18_	_43_ 44	31 _32_ 33
26 _27_	_20_ 21	17 _18_ 19
9 _10_	_7_ 8	40 _41_ 42
49 _50_	_32_ 33	26 _27_ 28

▶ Count the stacks of sea stars. Each stack has **10**.

| 10 | 10 | 10 | 10 | 10 | 10 | 10 | 10 | 10 | 10 |

▶ Connect the dots.
Start with **10**.

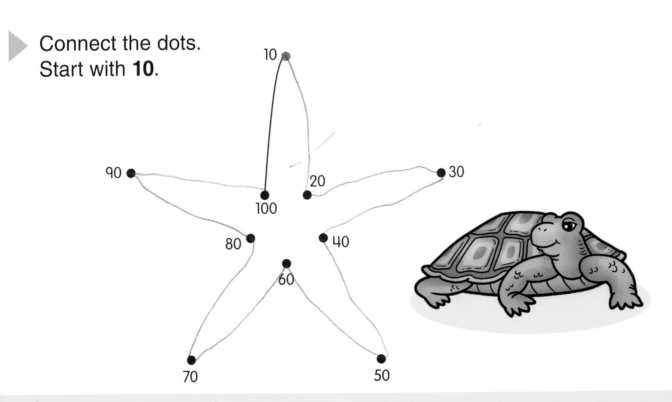

Count by 5s

▶ Each fish has five spots. Count by **5**s. Write the number.

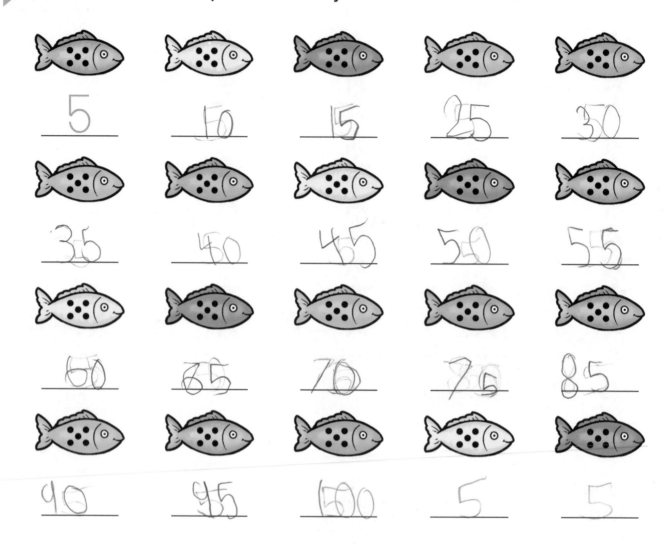

5   50   15   25   30

35   40   45   50   55

60   65   70   76   85

90   95   100   5   5

▶ Connect the dots. Count by **5**s.

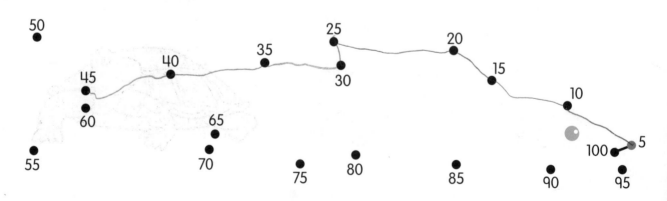

Jam and Jelly

▶ The jellyfish wants to eat jam. Count by **5**s to find the way.
Color the boxes.

5	10	15	20	80	20	78
25	13	60	25	54	9	66
41	40	35	30	31	38	4
90	45	34	29	57	4	41
36	50	5	80	85	90	27
22	55	66	75	72	95	1
26	60	65	70	50	100	88

JAM

Into the Ocean

Count by **5**s to get the crab back to the ocean.

EMC 4175 • © Evan-Moor Corp.

▶ Count the flip-flops by **2**s.

| 2 | 4 | 6 | 8 | 10 |

| 12 | 14 | 16 | 18 | 20 |

| 22 | 24 | 26 | 28 | 30 |

| 32 | 34 | 36 | 38 | 40 |

| 42 | 44 | 46 | 48 | 50 |

Race at Sea

▶ The sailboat wants to win the race.
Count by **2**s to find the way.
Color the boxes.

2	4	6	3	9	11	0
13	17	8	16	11	19	6
14	12	10	21	38	40	42
16	13	23	34	36	24	44
18	20	31	32	35	25	46
19	22	27	30	39	27	48
21	24	26	28	37	16	WINNER! 50

▶ Find the answers.

$$\begin{array}{r} 2 \\ +2 \\ \hline 4 \end{array} \qquad \begin{array}{r} 6 \\ -3 \\ \hline 3 \end{array} \qquad \begin{array}{r} 4 \\ +1 \\ \hline 5 \end{array} \qquad \begin{array}{r} 8 \\ +2 \\ \hline 10 \end{array} \qquad \begin{array}{r} 3 \\ -1 \\ \hline 2 \end{array}$$

$$\begin{array}{r} 7 \\ -4 \\ \hline 3 \end{array} \qquad \begin{array}{r} 3 \\ +5 \\ \hline 8 \end{array} \qquad \begin{array}{r} 6 \\ -5 \\ \hline 1 \end{array} \qquad \begin{array}{r} 4 \\ +7 \\ \hline 11 \end{array} \qquad \begin{array}{r} 10 \\ -4 \\ \hline 6 \end{array}$$

$$\begin{array}{r} 4 \\ +6 \\ \hline 10 \end{array} \qquad \begin{array}{r} 8 \\ -5 \\ \hline 3 \end{array} \qquad \begin{array}{r} 4 \\ -2 \\ \hline 2 \end{array} \qquad \begin{array}{r} 9 \\ -3 \\ \hline 6 \end{array} \qquad \begin{array}{r} 3 \\ +7 \\ \hline 10 \end{array}$$

$$\begin{array}{r} 10 \\ -0 \\ \hline 10 \end{array} \qquad \begin{array}{r} 8 \\ -6 \\ \hline 2 \end{array} \qquad \begin{array}{r} 5 \\ -2 \\ \hline 3 \end{array} \qquad \begin{array}{r} 7 \\ +2 \\ \hline 9 \end{array} \qquad \begin{array}{r} 6 \\ +4 \\ \hline 10 \end{array}$$

Under the Sea

▶ Find the answers.
Use the code to name the sea animals.

$\begin{array}{r} 4 \\ +4 \\ \hline \boxed{8} \end{array}$ $\begin{array}{r} 10 \\ -9 \\ \hline \boxed{1} \end{array}$ $\begin{array}{r} 3 \\ +2 \\ \hline \boxed{5} \end{array}$ $\begin{array}{r} 8 \\ -5 \\ \hline \boxed{3} \end{array}$	1 = a 4 = l 7 = r 2 = e 5 = n 8 = s 3 = d 6 = o 9 = t

__s__ __a__ __h__ __d__

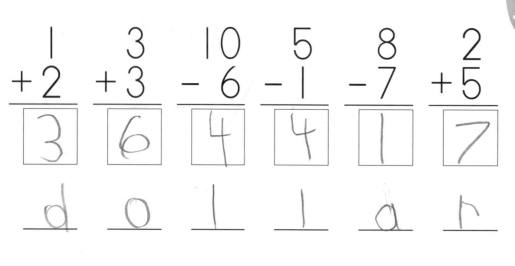

$\begin{array}{r} 1 \\ +2 \\ \hline \boxed{3} \end{array}$ $\begin{array}{r} 3 \\ +3 \\ \hline \boxed{6} \end{array}$ $\begin{array}{r} 10 \\ -6 \\ \hline \boxed{4} \end{array}$ $\begin{array}{r} 5 \\ -1 \\ \hline \boxed{4} \end{array}$ $\begin{array}{r} 8 \\ -7 \\ \hline \boxed{1} \end{array}$ $\begin{array}{r} 2 \\ +5 \\ \hline \boxed{7} \end{array}$

__d__ __o__ __l__ __l__ __a__ __r__

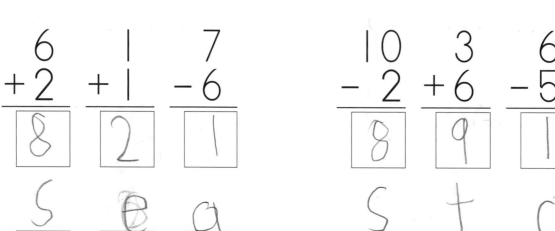

$\begin{array}{r} 6 \\ +2 \\ \hline \boxed{8} \end{array}$ $\begin{array}{r} 1 \\ +1 \\ \hline \boxed{2} \end{array}$ $\begin{array}{r} 7 \\ -6 \\ \hline \boxed{1} \end{array}$ $\begin{array}{r} 10 \\ -2 \\ \hline \boxed{8} \end{array}$ $\begin{array}{r} 3 \\ +6 \\ \hline \boxed{9} \end{array}$ $\begin{array}{r} 6 \\ -5 \\ \hline \boxed{1} \end{array}$ $\begin{array}{r} 8 \\ -1 \\ \hline \boxed{9} \end{array}$

__s__ __e__ __a__   __s__ __t__ __a__ __r__

EMC 4175 • © Evan-Moor Corp.

Sarah Ezzahir

Number Names

▶ Write the number names.

0 zero	**3** three	**6** six	**9** nine	**12** twelve
1 one	**4** four	**7** seven	**10** ten	**2** two
5 five	**8** eight	**11** eleven		

0 zero   6 six

3 three   12 twelve

5 five   1 one

9 nine   10 ten

11 eleven   4 four

2 two   7 seven

8 eight

Word Search

▶ Find the hidden numbers.
Circle them.

zero   three   six   nine   twelve
one   four   seven   ten   two
five   eight   eleven

```
n  o  n  e  s  i  x  g  d  w
o  h  z  e  r  o  o  f  i  c
h  e  i  g  h  t  u  x  r  p
t  h  r  e  e  v  s  m  o  n
t  e  n  e  t  w  e  l  v  e
f  o  u  r  s  e  v  e  n  g
n  i  n  e  g  d  d  s  m  l
t  w  o  y  c  f  i  v  e  x
e  l  e  v  e  n  n  v  s  k
```

Number Names

▶ Write the name for each number.

~~zero~~	three	nine	~~twelve~~
one	four	seven	ten
five	eight	~~eleven~~	two

Across
- ③ 7
- ④ 8
- ⑥ 4
- ⑦ 10
- ⑧ 12

Down
- ① 1
- ② 0
- ④ 11
- ⑤ 3
- ⑥ 5
- ⑧ 2

▶ Which number from the box is not in the puzzle?

_____

① o
n
② z
③ s e v e n
e
r
o
④ e l e v e ⑤ e
n
⑥ f o u r
⑦ t e n
f
i
⑧ t w e l v e
w
v
o
e

Crab Maze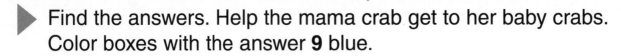

▶ Find the answers. Help the mama crab get to her baby crabs.
Color boxes with the answer **9** blue.

$\begin{array}{r} 7 \\ +2 \\ \hline 9 \end{array}$	$\begin{array}{r} 8 \\ +4 \\ \hline 12 \end{array}$	$\begin{array}{r} 9 \\ +5 \\ \hline 54 \end{array}$	$\begin{array}{r} 10 \\ +5 \\ \hline 15 \end{array}$	$\begin{array}{r} 14 \\ -9 \\ \hline 5 \end{array}$
$\begin{array}{r} 11 \\ -6 \\ \hline 5 \end{array}$	$\begin{array}{r} 12 \\ -3 \\ \hline 9 \end{array}$	$\begin{array}{r} 13 \\ -3 \\ \hline 10 \end{array}$	$\begin{array}{r} 6 \\ +9 \\ \hline 15 \end{array}$	$\begin{array}{r} 14 \\ -7 \\ \hline 8 \end{array}$	$\begin{array}{r} 7 \\ +5 \\ \hline 12 \end{array}$
$\begin{array}{r} 12 \\ -0 \\ \hline 12 \end{array}$	$\begin{array}{r} 15 \\ -6 \\ \hline 9 \end{array}$	$\begin{array}{r} 5 \\ +4 \\ \hline 9 \end{array}$	$\begin{array}{r} 8 \\ +6 \\ \hline \end{array}$	$\begin{array}{r} 5 \\ +9 \\ \hline \end{array}$	$\begin{array}{r} 15 \\ -8 \\ \hline \end{array}$
$\begin{array}{r} 11 \\ -7 \\ \hline \end{array}$	$\begin{array}{r} 8 \\ +5 \\ \hline \end{array}$	$\begin{array}{r} 14 \\ -5 \\ \hline 9 \end{array}$	$\begin{array}{r} 8 \\ +3 \\ \hline \end{array}$	$\begin{array}{r} 15 \\ -5 \\ \hline \end{array}$	$\begin{array}{r} 7 \\ +8 \\ \hline \end{array}$
$\begin{array}{r} 7 \\ +4 \\ \hline \end{array}$	$\begin{array}{r} 12 \\ -7 \\ \hline \end{array}$	$\begin{array}{r} 11 \\ -2 \\ \hline 9 \end{array}$	$\begin{array}{r} 13 \\ -4 \\ \hline 9 \end{array}$	$\begin{array}{r} 6 \\ +3 \\ \hline 9 \end{array}$	

EMC 4175 • © Evan-Moor Corp.

▶ Find the answers. Color the fish.

7 yellow	9 orange	14 red
8 green	12 purple	16 blue

$16 - 8 =$ 8  $9 + 7 =$ 16

$14 - 5 =$ 9  $14 - 7 =$ 8

$8 + 8 =$ 16  $6 + 6 =$ 12

$9 + 3 =$ 12  $12 - 4 =$ 8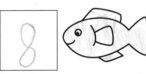

$10 + 4 =$ 14 $18 - 9 =$ 8

Who Am I?

▶ Find the answers.
Use the code to name the mystery animal.

12 = a	
13 = b	
14 = e	
15 = h	
16 = l	
17 = u	
18 = w	

$$\begin{array}{r} 6 \\ +6 \\ \hline \boxed{12} \\ a \end{array}$$

$$\begin{array}{r} 9 \\ +4 \\ \hline \boxed{13} \\ b \end{array}$$

$$\begin{array}{r} 8 \\ +8 \\ \hline \boxed{16} \\ l \end{array}$$

$$\begin{array}{r} 9 \\ +8 \\ \hline \boxed{17} \\ w \end{array}$$

$$\begin{array}{r} 7 \\ +7 \\ \hline \boxed{14} \\ e \end{array}$$

$$\begin{array}{r} 9 \\ +9 \\ \hline \boxed{18} \\ w \end{array}$$

$$\begin{array}{r} 6 \\ +9 \\ \hline \boxed{15} \\ h \end{array}$$

$$\begin{array}{r} 5 \\ +7 \\ \hline \boxed{12} \\ a \end{array}$$

$$\begin{array}{r} 7 \\ +9 \\ \hline \boxed{16} \\ l \end{array}$$

$$\begin{array}{r} 5 \\ +9 \\ \hline \boxed{14} \\ e \end{array}$$

▶ Draw the
mystery animal.

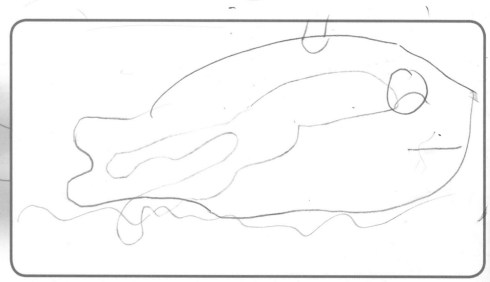

EMC 4175 • © Evan-Moor Corp.

Fact families have **2** addition sentences and **2** subtraction sentences made from **3** numbers. Complete each fact family.

2   8   10

$$2 + 8 = 10$$
$$8 + 2 = 10$$
$$10 - 2 = 8$$
$$10 - 8 = 2$$

9   5   14

$$9 + 5 = 14$$
$$5 + 9 = 14$$
$$14 - 5 = 9$$
$$14 - 9 = 5$$

6   7   13

$$6 + 7 = 13$$
$$7 + 6 = 13$$
$$13 - 6 = 7$$
$$13 - 7 = 6$$

8   4   12

$$8 + 4 = 12$$
$$4 + 8 = 12$$
$$12 - 8 = 4$$
$$12 - 4 = 8$$

Treasure Chest

▶ How much money is in each?

 43 ¢

 20 ¢

 12 ¢

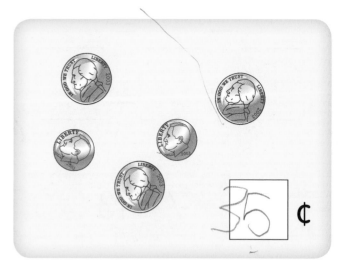 35 ¢

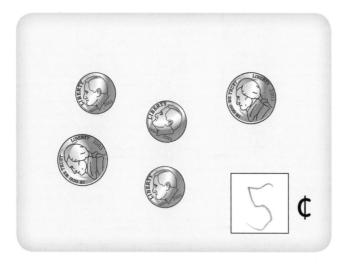 5 ¢

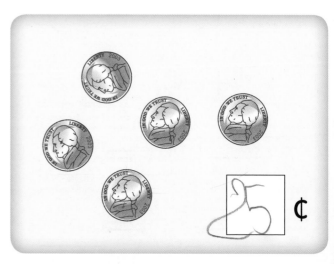 25 ¢

EMC 4175 • © Evan-Moor Corp.

Where Do Pet Fish Live?

▶ Connect the dots. Start with **one**.

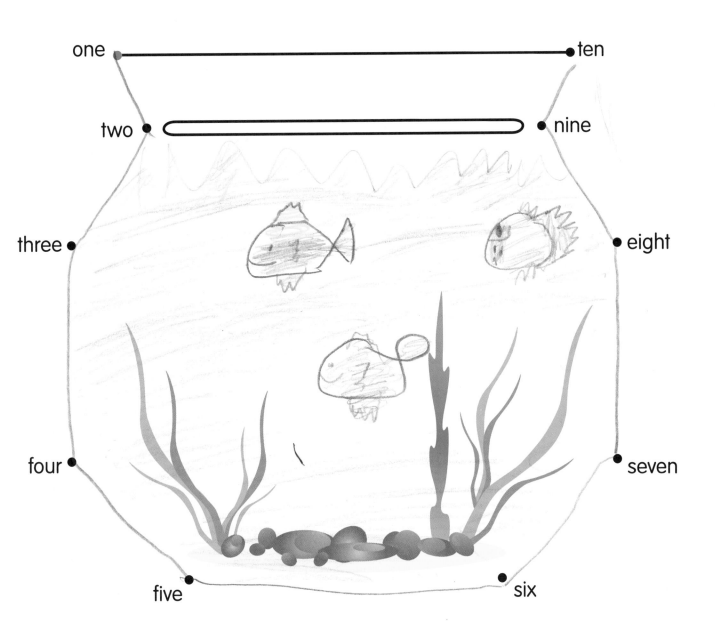

▶ Draw three fish and one snail in the bowl.

Name the Shapes

▶ Find the answers.
Use the code to name the shapes.

$$12 - 3 = \boxed{9} \quad 6 + 6 = \boxed{12} \quad 1 - 0 = \boxed{1} \quad 13 - 6 = \boxed{7}$$

o   v   a   l

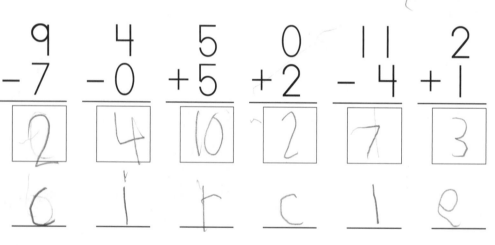

$$9 - 7 = \boxed{2} \quad 4 - 0 = \boxed{4} \quad 5 + 5 = \boxed{10} \quad 0 + 2 = \boxed{2} \quad 11 - 4 = \boxed{7} \quad 2 + 1 = \boxed{3}$$

c   i   r   c   l   e

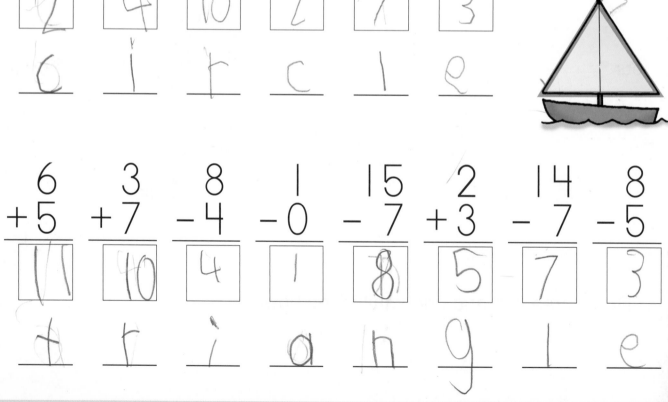

$$6 + 5 = \boxed{11} \quad 3 + 7 = \boxed{10} \quad 8 - 4 = \boxed{4} \quad 1 - 0 = \boxed{1} \quad 15 - 7 = \boxed{8} \quad 2 + 3 = \boxed{5} \quad 14 - 7 = \boxed{7} \quad 8 - 5 = \boxed{3}$$

t   r   i   a   n   g   l   e

22

Word Search

Find the hidden shape names.
Circle them.

○ circle   ▭ rectangle   ☆ star

▢ square   ⬠ pentagon   ♡ heart

△ triangle   ⬭ oval   ⬡ hexagon

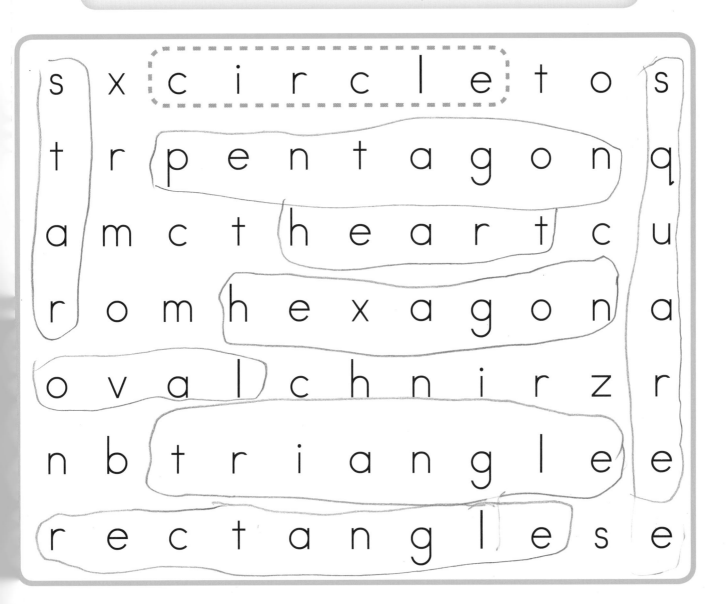

```
s  x  c  i  r  c  l  e  t  o  s
t  r  p  e  n  t  a  g  o  n  q
a  m  c  t  h  e  a  r  t  c  u
r  o  m  h  e  x  a  g  o  n  a
o  v  a  l  c  h  n  i  r  z  r
n  b  t  r  i  a  n  g  l  e  e
r  e  c  t  a  n  g  l  e  s  e
```

Symmetry

▶ Draw the other side. Make both sides the same.

▶ The children went fishing on Saturday.
Use the graph to answer the questions.

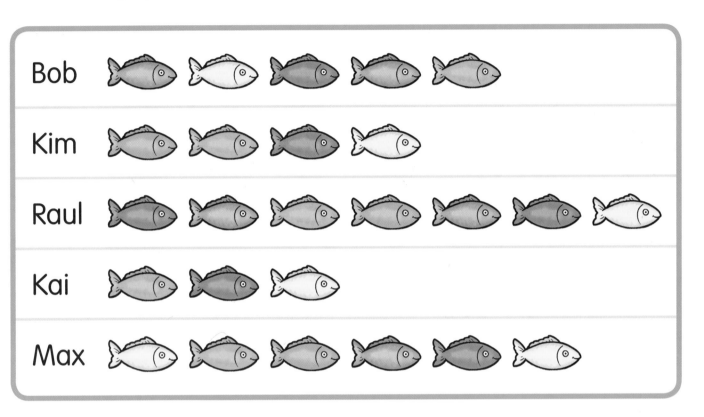

Bob	🐟🐟🐟🐟🐟
Kim	🐟🐟🐟🐟
Raul	🐟🐟🐟🐟🐟🐟🐟
Kai	🐟🐟🐟
Max	🐟🐟🐟🐟🐟🐟

1. How many fish did each child catch?

Bob __5__   Kim __4__   Raul __7__

Kai __3__   Max __6__

2. Who caught the most? __Raul__

3. Who caught the fewest? __Kai__

4. How many more fish did Raul catch than Kai? __4__

50 to 100

▶ Connect the dots.
Start with **50**.

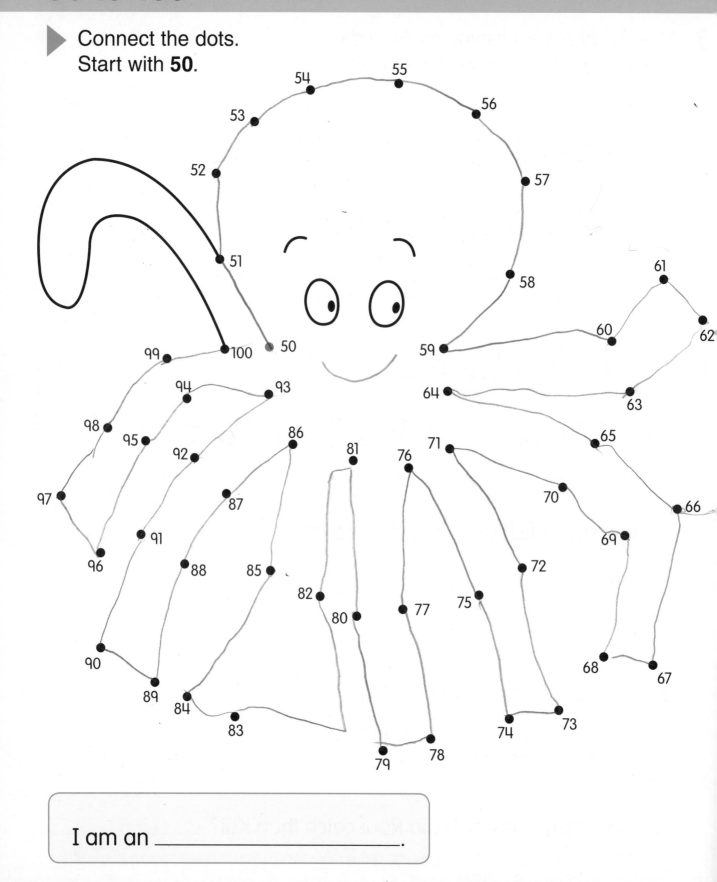

I am an _____.

Read and follow the directions.

1. Start at the .

2. Go right **3** boxes. What do you see? _turtle_

3. Go down **2** boxes. What do you see? _crab_

4. Go right **3** boxes. What do you see? _fish_

5. Go up **4** boxes. What do you see? _octopus_

Mystery Picture

Add and subtract.
Color.

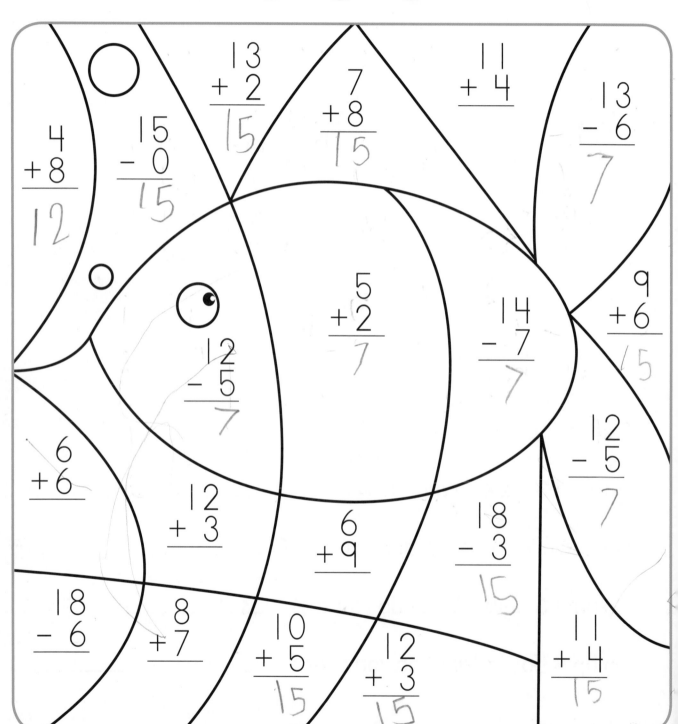

Count to 100

Write the numbers **1** to **100** in order.

1	2	3	4	5	6	7	8	9	10
11	12	13	14	15	16	17	18	19	20
21	22	23	24	25	26	27	28	29	30
31	32	33	34	35	36	37	38	39	40
41	42	43	44	45	46	47	48	49	50
51	52	53	54	55	56	57	58	59	60
61	62	63	64	65	66	67	68	69	70
71	72	73	74	75	76	77	78	79	80
81	82	83	84	85	86	87	88	89	90
91	92	93	94	95	96	97	98	99	100

Count by 2s

▶ Connect the dots. Start with **2**. Count by **2s**.

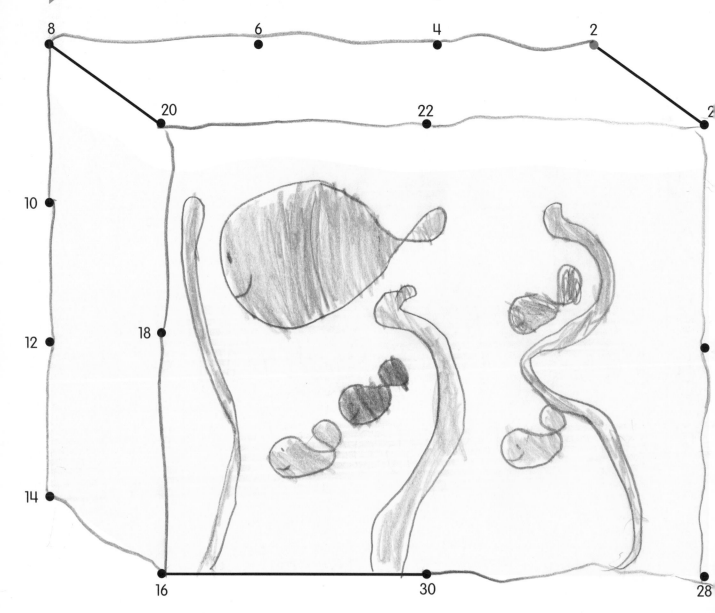

▶ Follow the directions.

1. Draw **1** big fish and **4** small fish in the aquarium.

2. Draw **2** snails.

3. Draw **3** water plants.

EMC 4175 • © Evan-Moor Corp.

Add and Subtract

Write the problems. Find the answers.

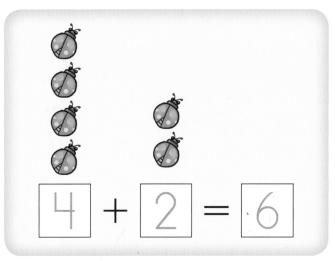

$$4 + 2 = 6$$

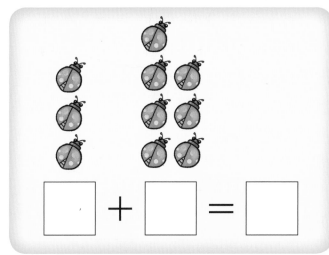

$$\boxed{} + \boxed{} = \boxed{}$$

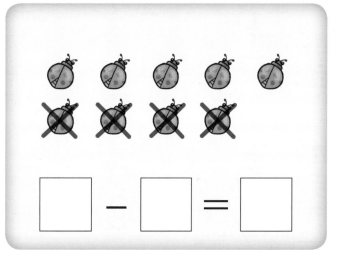

$$\boxed{} - \boxed{} = \boxed{}$$

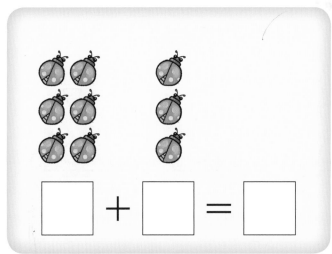

$$\boxed{} + \boxed{} = \boxed{}$$

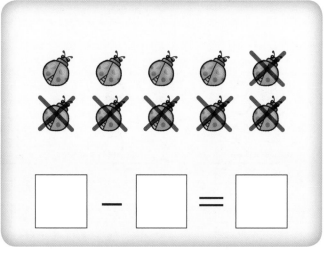

$$\boxed{} - \boxed{} = \boxed{}$$

Add and Subtract

▶ Find the answers.

$$\begin{array}{r} 2 \\ +2 \\ \hline \boxed{4} \end{array} \qquad \begin{array}{r} 8 \\ -4 \\ \hline \boxed{4} \end{array} \qquad \begin{array}{r} 0 \\ +9 \\ \hline \boxed{9} \end{array} \qquad \begin{array}{r} 4 \\ +3 \\ \hline \boxed{7} \end{array} \qquad \begin{array}{r} 6 \\ -5 \\ \hline \boxed{1} \end{array}$$

$$\begin{array}{r} 1 \\ +8 \\ \hline \boxed{9} \end{array} \qquad \begin{array}{r} 5 \\ -3 \\ \hline \boxed{2} \end{array} \qquad \begin{array}{r} 7 \\ +2 \\ \hline \boxed{9} \end{array} \qquad \begin{array}{r} 3 \\ +4 \\ \hline \boxed{7} \end{array} \qquad \begin{array}{r} 4 \\ -2 \\ \hline \boxed{2} \end{array}$$

$$\begin{array}{r} 5 \\ +1 \\ \hline \boxed{6} \end{array} \qquad \begin{array}{r} 6 \\ +2 \\ \hline \boxed{8} \end{array} \qquad \begin{array}{r} 9 \\ -5 \\ \hline \boxed{4} \end{array} \qquad \begin{array}{r} 2 \\ -1 \\ \hline \boxed{1} \end{array} \qquad \begin{array}{r} 5 \\ +4 \\ \hline \boxed{9} \end{array}$$

$$\begin{array}{r} 8 \\ -2 \\ \hline \boxed{6} \end{array} \qquad \begin{array}{r} 9 \\ -6 \\ \hline \boxed{3} \end{array} \qquad \begin{array}{r} 5 \\ +5 \\ \hline \boxed{10} \end{array} \qquad \begin{array}{r} 3 \\ +3 \\ \hline \boxed{6} \end{array} \qquad \begin{array}{r} 7 \\ -6 \\ \hline \boxed{1} \end{array}$$

EMC 4175 • © Evan-Moor Corp.

▶ Check your subtraction by adding.

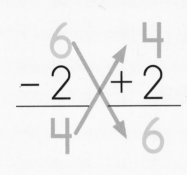

$$\begin{array}{cc} 9 & \boxed{3} \\ -6 & +6 \\ \hline \boxed{3} & \boxed{9} \end{array}$$

$$\begin{array}{cc} 10 & \boxed{3} \\ -7 & +7 \\ \hline \boxed{3} & \boxed{10} \end{array}$$

$$\begin{array}{cc} 8 & \boxed{2} \\ -6 & +6 \\ \hline \boxed{2} & \boxed{8} \end{array}$$

$$\begin{array}{cc} 7 & \boxed{5} \\ -2 & +2 \\ \hline \boxed{5} & \boxed{7} \end{array}$$

$$\begin{array}{cc} 10 & \boxed{8} \\ -3 & +3 \\ \hline \boxed{8} & \boxed{10} \end{array}$$

$$\begin{array}{cc} 7 & \boxed{6} \\ -1 & +1 \\ \hline \boxed{6} & \boxed{7} \end{array}$$

$$\begin{array}{cc} 6 & \boxed{2} \\ -4 & +4 \\ \hline \boxed{2} & \boxed{6} \end{array}$$

$$\begin{array}{cc} 9 & \boxed{6} \\ -3 & +3 \\ \hline \boxed{6} & \boxed{9} \end{array}$$

Add the Numbers

▶ Find the answers.

$$\begin{array}{r} 4 \\ 2 \\ + 1 \\ \hline \boxed{7} \end{array}$$

$$\begin{array}{r} 5 \\ 3 \\ + 2 \\ \hline \boxed{10} \end{array}$$

$$\begin{array}{r} 2 \\ 2 \\ + 2 \\ \hline \boxed{6} \end{array}$$

$$\begin{array}{r} 6 \\ 1 \\ + 4 \\ \hline \boxed{15} \end{array}$$

$$\begin{array}{r} 3 \\ 0 \\ + 5 \\ \hline \boxed{8} \end{array} \qquad \begin{array}{r} 1 \\ 4 \\ + 4 \\ \hline \boxed{9} \end{array} \qquad \begin{array}{r} 6 \\ 6 \\ + 1 \\ \hline \boxed{13} \end{array} \qquad \begin{array}{r} 2 \\ 7 \\ + 1 \\ \hline \boxed{10} \end{array} \qquad \begin{array}{r} 6 \\ 1 \\ + 4 \\ \hline \boxed{45} \end{array}$$

EMC 4175 • © Evan-Moor Corp.

Ladybugs Everywhere

▶ Add or subtract.

Color the bugs with the answer **5**

 0+1  5+0  3−3  6−1

Color the bugs with the answer **7**

 9−2 7+2  4+3 7−0

Color the bugs with the answer **3**

 4−2 6−3  9−6 9+1

Color the bugs with the answer **8**

 4+4 6−6  3+5 8−2

Fact Families

▶ Use the numbers to make fact families.

5   4   9

$5 + 4 = 9$

$4 + 5 = 9$

$9 - 5 = 4$

$5 - 9 = 4$

6   4   10

$6 + 4 = 10$

$4 + 6 = 10$

$10 - 6 = 4$

$10 - 4 = 6$

3   5   8

$3 + 5 = 8$

$5 + 3 = 8$

$8 - 5 = 3$

$8 - 3 = 5$

5   2   7

$5 + 2 = 7$

$2 + 5 = 2$

$7 - 5 = 2$

$7 - 2 = 5$

EMC 4175 • © Evan-Moor Corp.

Add and Subtract

▶ Write the problems. Find the answers.

| 3 | + | 8 | = | 11 |

| 10 | − | 5 | = | 5 |

| 3 | + | 9 | = | 12 |

| 12 | − | 4 | = | 8 |

| 5 | + | 5 | = | 10 |

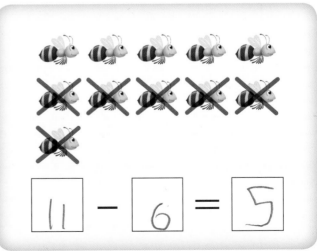

| 11 | − | 6 | = | 5 |

Add and Subtract

▶ Find the answers.

$$
\begin{array}{r} 7 \\ +3 \\ \hline \boxed{10} \end{array}
\qquad
\begin{array}{r} 8 \\ +4 \\ \hline \boxed{12} \end{array}
\qquad
\begin{array}{r} 12 \\ -3 \\ \hline \boxed{9} \end{array}
\qquad
\begin{array}{r} 14 \\ -9 \\ \hline \boxed{5} \end{array}
\qquad
\begin{array}{r} 10 \\ -7 \\ \hline \boxed{3} \end{array}
$$

$$
\begin{array}{r} 10 \\ -8 \\ \hline \boxed{4} \end{array}
\qquad
\begin{array}{r} 14 \\ -3 \\ \hline \boxed{11} \end{array}
\qquad
\begin{array}{r} 3 \\ +9 \\ \hline \boxed{12} \end{array}
\qquad
\begin{array}{r} 10 \\ -6 \\ \hline \boxed{4} \end{array}
\qquad
\begin{array}{r} 4 \\ +7 \\ \hline \boxed{11} \end{array}
$$

$$
\begin{array}{r} 6 \\ +6 \\ \hline \boxed{12} \end{array}
\qquad
\begin{array}{r} 12 \\ -9 \\ \hline \boxed{3} \end{array}
\qquad
\begin{array}{r} 10 \\ -0 \\ \hline \boxed{10} \end{array}
\qquad
\begin{array}{r} 5 \\ +6 \\ \hline \boxed{11} \end{array}
\qquad
\begin{array}{r} 11 \\ -8 \\ \hline \boxed{3} \end{array}
$$

$$
\begin{array}{r} 12 \\ -9 \\ \hline \boxed{4} \end{array}
\qquad
\begin{array}{r} 8 \\ +3 \\ \hline \boxed{11} \end{array}
\qquad
\begin{array}{r} 7 \\ +5 \\ \hline \boxed{12} \end{array}
\qquad
\begin{array}{r} 11 \\ -2 \\ \hline \boxed{9} \end{array}
\qquad
\begin{array}{r} 12 \\ -8 \\ \hline \boxed{4} \end{array}
$$

Write the problems. Find the answers.

$$4 + 9 = 13$$

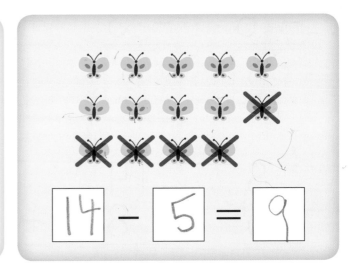

$$13 - 7 = 6$$

$$6 + 8 = 14$$

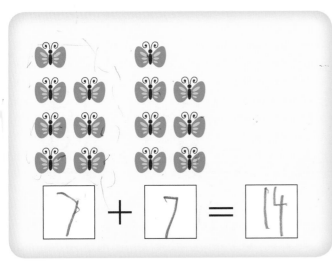

$$14 - 5 = 9$$

$$7 + 7 = 14$$

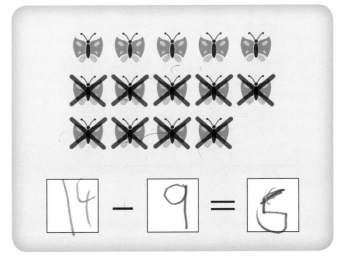

$$14 - 9 = 5$$

Add and Subtract

▶ Find the answers.

$$\begin{array}{r} 5 \\ +8 \\ \hline \boxed{13} \end{array} \qquad \begin{array}{r} 6 \\ +4 \\ \hline \boxed{10} \end{array} \qquad \begin{array}{r} 12 \\ -5 \\ \hline \boxed{7} \end{array} \qquad \begin{array}{r} 13 \\ -4 \\ \hline \boxed{9} \end{array} \qquad \begin{array}{r} 7 \\ +6 \\ \hline \boxed{1} \end{array}$$

$$\begin{array}{r} 14 \\ -6 \\ \hline \boxed{8} \end{array} \qquad \begin{array}{r} 10 \\ -3 \\ \hline \boxed{7} \end{array} \qquad \begin{array}{r} 4 \\ +8 \\ \hline \boxed{12} \end{array} \qquad \begin{array}{r} 11 \\ -9 \\ \hline \boxed{2} \end{array} \qquad \begin{array}{r} 6 \\ +7 \\ \hline \boxed{13} \end{array}$$

$$\begin{array}{r} 8 \\ +5 \\ \hline \boxed{13} \end{array} \qquad \begin{array}{r} 14 \\ -8 \\ \hline \boxed{6} \end{array} \qquad \begin{array}{r} 9 \\ +4 \\ \hline \boxed{13} \end{array} \qquad \begin{array}{r} 13 \\ -6 \\ \hline \boxed{7} \end{array} \qquad \begin{array}{r} 13 \\ -7 \\ \hline \boxed{16} \end{array}$$

$$\begin{array}{r} 12 \\ -9 \\ \hline \boxed{3} \end{array} \qquad \begin{array}{r} 14 \\ -7 \\ \hline \boxed{7} \end{array} \qquad \begin{array}{r} 14 \\ -0 \\ \hline \boxed{14} \end{array} \qquad \begin{array}{r} 13 \\ -9 \\ \hline \boxed{4} \end{array} \qquad \begin{array}{r} 14 \\ -9 \\ \hline \boxed{5} \end{array}$$

How Many Ways?

► Circle the numbers.

Circle ways to make **9**	Circle ways to make **10**	Circle ways to make **11**
(13 – 4)	4 + 9	4 + 7
12 – 5	(12 – 2)	12 – 6
(6 + 3)	3 + 7	5 + 6
(9 – 0)	13 – 3	12 – 4
(11 – 2)	11 – 1	(11 – 0)
13 – 5	6 + 4	9 + 2

Circle ways to make **12**	Circle ways to make **13**	Circle ways to make **14**
8 + 4	(11 + 2)	(7 + 7)
12 – 4	12 – 9	(15 – 1)
5 + 7	(6 + 7)	(9 + 5)
9 – 3	(10 + 3)	(13 + 1)
(12 – 0)	(13 – 0)	(14 – 0)
6 + 6	4 + 9	(6 + 8)

Add and Subtract

▶ Write the problems. Find the answers.

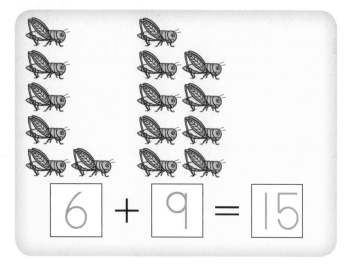

$$6 + 9 = 15$$

$$16 - 8 = 7$$

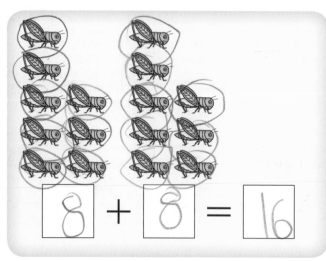

$$8 + 8 = 16$$

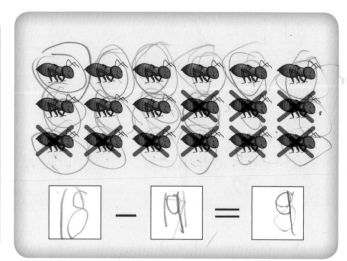

$$18 - 9 = 9$$

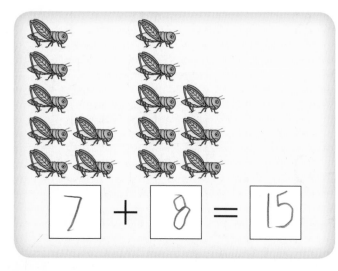

$$7 + 8 = 15$$

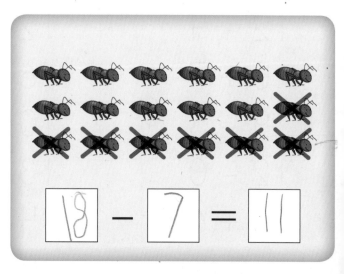

$$18 - 7 = 11$$

EMC 4175 • © Evan-Moor Corp.

Add and Subtract

Find the answers.

6 +9 **15**	9 +8 ☐	16 −9 ☐	18 −9 ☐	17 +0 ☐

15 −7 ☐	7 +9 ☐	15 −9 ☐	17 −9 ☐	18 −8 ☐

9 +9 ☐	17 −8 ☐	8 +5 ☐	18 −9 ☐	10 +2 ☐

9 bees were in the hive. 8 more came. How many bees were in the hive?

_____ bees

15 eggs were in the hive. 7 eggs hatched. How many did not hatch?

_____ eggs

Riddles

▶ Use the code to solve the riddles.
Write the matching letter below each answer.

b = 7	e = 8	h = 9	i = 10
n = 11	o = 12	v = 13	y = 14

What is black and yellow and buzzes?

$$\begin{array}{r} 15 \\ -\ 6 \\ \hline \boxed{9} \end{array} \quad \begin{array}{r} 6 \\ +6 \\ \hline \Box \end{array} \quad \begin{array}{r} 4 \\ +7 \\ \hline \Box \end{array} \quad \begin{array}{r} 9 \\ -\ 1 \\ \hline \Box \end{array} \quad \begin{array}{r} 8 \\ +6 \\ \hline \Box \end{array} \quad \begin{array}{r} 16 \\ -\ 9 \\ \hline \Box \end{array} \quad \begin{array}{r} 5 \\ +3 \\ \hline \Box \end{array} \quad \begin{array}{r} 16 \\ -\ 8 \\ \hline \Box \end{array}$$

___ ___ ___ ___ ___ ___ ___ ___

Where does it live?

$$\begin{array}{r} 18 \\ -\ 9 \\ \hline \Box \end{array} \quad \begin{array}{r} 7 \\ +3 \\ \hline \Box \end{array} \quad \begin{array}{r} 8 \\ +5 \\ \hline \Box \end{array} \quad \begin{array}{r} 14 \\ -\ 6 \\ \hline \Box \end{array}$$

___ ___ ___ ___

Draw the answer here.

EMC 4175 • © Evan-Moor Corp.

Flying Home

Show the bee the way to the hive. Find the answers.
Color the boxes that equal **9** green.

$\begin{matrix} 11 \\ -\ 7 \\ \hline \end{matrix}$	$\begin{matrix} 10 \\ +\ 5 \\ \hline \end{matrix}$	$\begin{matrix} 12 \\ -\ 2 \\ \hline \end{matrix}$	$\begin{matrix} 15 \\ -\ 6 \\ \hline 9 \end{matrix}$	
$\begin{matrix} 12 \\ -\ 3 \\ \hline \end{matrix}$	$\begin{matrix} 9 \\ +0 \\ \hline \end{matrix}$	$\begin{matrix} 5 \\ +4 \\ \hline \end{matrix}$	$\begin{matrix} 14 \\ -\ 5 \\ \hline \end{matrix}$	$\begin{matrix} 5 \\ +9 \\ \hline \end{matrix}$
$\begin{matrix} 11 \\ -\ 2 \\ \hline \end{matrix}$	$\begin{matrix} 7 \\ +5 \\ \hline \end{matrix}$	$\begin{matrix} 10 \\ +\ 3 \\ \hline \end{matrix}$	$\begin{matrix} 4 \\ +7 \\ \hline \end{matrix}$	$\begin{matrix} 13 \\ -\ 5 \\ \hline \end{matrix}$
$\begin{matrix} 13 \\ -\ 4 \\ \hline \end{matrix}$	$\begin{matrix} 6 \\ +3 \\ \hline \end{matrix}$	$\begin{matrix} 2 \\ +7 \\ \hline \end{matrix}$	$\begin{matrix} 13 \\ -\ 6 \\ \hline \end{matrix}$	$\begin{matrix} 4 \\ +9 \\ \hline \end{matrix}$
$\begin{matrix} 9 \\ +2 \\ \hline \end{matrix}$	$\begin{matrix} 8 \\ +3 \\ \hline \end{matrix}$	$\begin{matrix} 10 \\ -\ 1 \\ \hline \end{matrix}$	$\begin{matrix} 16 \\ -\ 7 \\ \hline \end{matrix}$	

Caterpillars

▶ Add the numbers on each caterpillar.

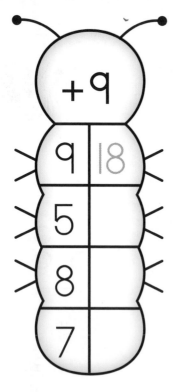

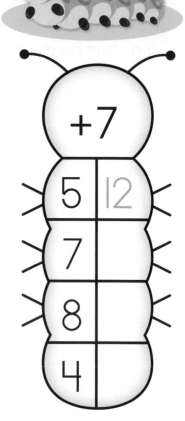

▶ Subtract the numbers on each caterpillar.

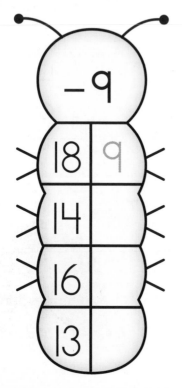
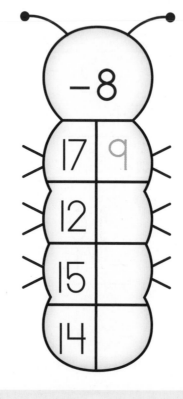
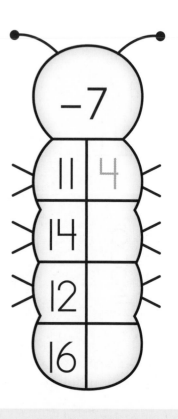

EMC 4175 • © Evan-Moor Corp.

Plus or Minus

Write the missing **+** or **–** signs.

9 **+** 9 18	8 ☐ 6 14	16 ☐ 9 7	13 ☐ 7 6
8 ☐ 5 13	18 ☐ 9 9	15 ☐ 7 8	7 ☐ 7 14
8 ☐ 8 16	13 ☐ 4 9	15 ☐ 6 9	6 ☐ 8 14
17 ☐ 9 8	5 ☐ 7 12	15 ☐ 9 6	7 ☐ 8 15

Find the Pattern

▶ Add and subtract. Then color the boxes.

| 9 = red | 8 = purple | 7 = yellow |

18 − 9 9	12 − 4	12 − 5	6 + 3	16 − 8
4 + 3	15 − 6	4 + 4	7 + 0	8 + 1
8 + 0	16 − 9	12 − 3	11 − 3	11 − 4
7 + 2	5 + 3	10 − 3	14 − 5	10 − 2
1 + 6	17 − 8	1 + 7	14 − 7	5 + 4

Find the answers to help the grasshopper get to the grass.

$$10 - 5 = \boxed{5}$$

$$8 + 2 = \boxed{}$$

$$14 - 7 = \boxed{}$$

$$6 + 9 = \boxed{}$$

$$15 - 8 = \boxed{}$$

$$11 - 8 = \boxed{}$$

$$9 + 8 = \boxed{}$$

$$15 - 6 = \boxed{}$$

$$12 - 8 = \boxed{}$$

$$5 + 7 = \boxed{}$$

$$8 + 9 = \boxed{}$$

$$18 - 9 = \boxed{}$$

Ladybugs

▶ Color the ladybugs with the same answers the same color.

$$\begin{array}{r} 6 \\ + 6 \\ \hline 12 \end{array}$$

$$\begin{array}{r} 15 \\ - 6 \\ \hline \end{array}$$

$$\begin{array}{r} 5 \\ + 3 \\ \hline \end{array}$$

$$\begin{array}{r} 7 \\ + 7 \\ \hline \end{array}$$

$$\begin{array}{r} 18 \\ - 9 \\ \hline \end{array}$$

$$\begin{array}{r} 4 \\ + 4 \\ \hline \end{array}$$

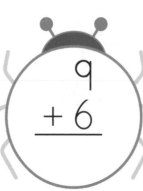

$$\begin{array}{r} 9 \\ + 6 \\ \hline \end{array}$$

$$\begin{array}{r} 12 \\ - 7 \\ \hline \end{array}$$

$$\begin{array}{r} 8 \\ + 7 \\ \hline \end{array}$$

$$\begin{array}{r} 9 \\ + 3 \\ \hline 12 \end{array}$$

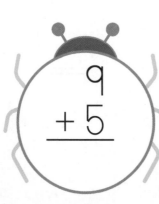

$$\begin{array}{r} 9 \\ + 5 \\ \hline \end{array}$$

$$\begin{array}{r} 11 \\ - 6 \\ \hline \end{array}$$

EMC 4175 • © Evan-Moor Corp.

Add the numbers that make **10**. Then add the last number.

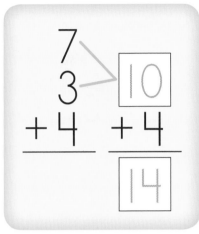

$$\begin{array}{r} 7 \\ 3 \\ +4 \\ \hline \end{array} \quad \begin{array}{r} 10 \\ +4 \\ \hline 14 \end{array}$$

$$\begin{array}{r} 1 \\ 9 \\ +2 \\ \hline \end{array} \quad \begin{array}{r} \square \\ +2 \\ \hline \square \end{array}$$

$$\begin{array}{r} 4 \\ 9 \\ +1 \\ \hline \end{array} \quad \begin{array}{r} \square \\ +4 \\ \hline \square \end{array}$$

Add the doubles. Then add the last number.

$$\begin{array}{r} 3 \\ 3 \\ +9 \\ \hline \end{array} \quad \begin{array}{r} \square \\ +9 \\ \hline \square \end{array}$$

$$\begin{array}{r} 2 \\ 2 \\ +8 \\ \hline \end{array} \quad \begin{array}{r} \square \\ +8 \\ \hline \square \end{array}$$

$$\begin{array}{r} 4 \\ 3 \\ +3 \\ \hline \end{array} \quad \begin{array}{r} \square \\ +4 \\ \hline \square \end{array}$$

Add all three numbers.

$$\begin{array}{r} 6 \\ 3 \\ +5 \\ \hline \square \end{array} \quad \begin{array}{r} 2 \\ 3 \\ +4 \\ \hline \square \end{array} \quad \begin{array}{r} 5 \\ 3 \\ +7 \\ \hline \square \end{array} \quad \begin{array}{r} 3 \\ 8 \\ +7 \\ \hline \square \end{array} \quad \begin{array}{r} 5 \\ 0 \\ +9 \\ \hline \square \end{array}$$

Fact Families

Use the numbers to make fact families.

9   6   15

9 + 6 = 15

___ + ___ = ___

___ − ___ = ___

___ − ___ = ___

7   6   13

___ + ___ = ___

___ + ___ = ___

___ − ___ = ___

___ − ___ = ___

5   7   12

___ + ___ = ___

___ + ___ = ___

___ − ___ = ___

___ − ___ = ___

8   6   14

___ + ___ = ___

___ + ___ = ___

___ − ___ = ___

___ − ___ = ___

▶ Find the answers.

> I know **6 + 3** is **9**,
> so **9 − 6** must be **3**.

$9 + 6 = 15$ **so** $15 - 9 = \boxed{6}$

$9 + 8 = 17$ **so** $17 - 9 = \boxed{}$

$4 + 6 = 10$ **so** $10 - 4 = \boxed{}$

$3 + 9 = 12$ **so** $12 - 3 = \boxed{}$

$8 + 5 = 13$ **so** $13 - 8 = \boxed{}$

> I know **10 − 9** is **1**,
> so **9 + 1** must be **10**.

$18 - 9 = 9$ **so** $9 + 9 = \boxed{18}$

$10 - 6 = 4$ **so** $6 + 4 = \boxed{}$

$15 - 6 = 9$ **so** $6 + 9 = \boxed{}$

$12 - 8 = 4$ **so** $8 + 4 = \boxed{}$

$17 - 8 = 9$ **so** $8 + 9 = \boxed{}$

How Many Tens?

▶ Circle groups of **10** insects. How many tens did you make? How many are left?

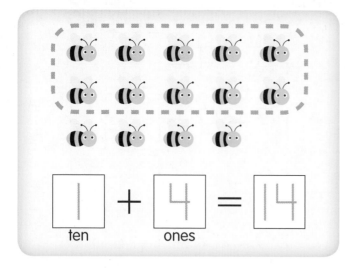

1	+	4	=	14
ten		ones		

	+		=
ten		ones	

	+		=
ten		ones	

	+		=
ten		ones	

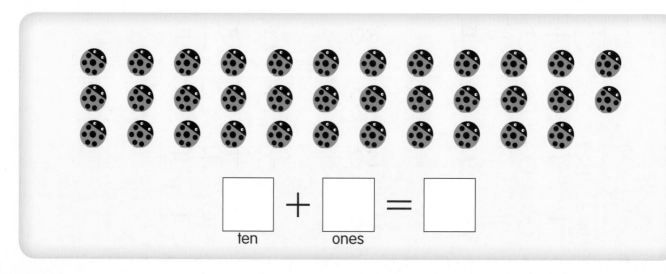

	+		=
ten		ones	

Add or subtract the **ones** first.
Then add or subtract the **tens**.

tens	ones
2	7
+3	0
5	7

tens	ones
9	8
−2	5

tens	ones
1	3
+3	1

tens	ones
6	4
−3	0

tens	ones
6	0
+2	5

tens	ones
3	7
−2	7

tens	ones
8	6
−7	5

tens	ones
7	1
−5	1

tens	ones
5	1
+4	4

Two-Digit Numbers

▶ Find the answers.

```
   23      10      67      59      35
 + 22    + 20    - 35    - 17    + 54
 ┌──┐    ┌──┐    ┌──┐    ┌──┐    ┌──┐
 │45│    │  │    │  │    │  │    │  │
 └──┘    └──┘    └──┘    └──┘    └──┘
```

```
   76      40      69      43      38
 - 32    +  7    - 23    + 34    - 16
 ┌──┐    ┌──┐    ┌──┐    ┌──┐    ┌──┐
 │  │    │  │    │  │    │  │    │  │
 └──┘    └──┘    └──┘    └──┘    └──┘
```

```
   23      88      69      98      45
 + 20    - 46    - 34    - 52    + 20
 ┌──┐    ┌──┐    ┌──┐    ┌──┐    ┌──┐
 │  │    │  │    │  │    │  │    │  │
 └──┘    └──┘    └──┘    └──┘    └──┘
```

```
   62      22      59      37      65
 + 34    - 11    - 46    + 21    + 34
 ┌──┐    ┌──┐    ┌──┐    ┌──┐    ┌──┐
 │  │    │  │    │  │    │  │    │  │
 └──┘    └──┘    └──┘    └──┘    └──┘
```

EMC 4175 • © Evan-Moor Corp.

Put an **X** on problems with the wrong answer.
Circle the problems that are correct.

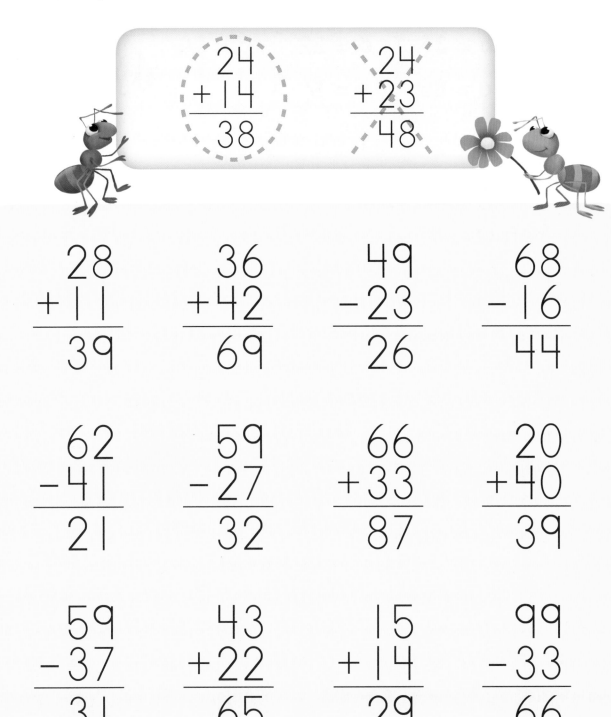

$$
\begin{array}{r} 24 \\ +14 \\ \hline 38 \end{array}
\qquad
\begin{array}{r} 24 \\ +23 \\ \hline 48 \end{array}
$$

$$
\begin{array}{r} 28 \\ +11 \\ \hline 39 \end{array}
\qquad
\begin{array}{r} 36 \\ +42 \\ \hline 69 \end{array}
\qquad
\begin{array}{r} 49 \\ -23 \\ \hline 26 \end{array}
\qquad
\begin{array}{r} 68 \\ -16 \\ \hline 44 \end{array}
$$

$$
\begin{array}{r} 62 \\ -41 \\ \hline 21 \end{array}
\qquad
\begin{array}{r} 59 \\ -27 \\ \hline 32 \end{array}
\qquad
\begin{array}{r} 66 \\ +33 \\ \hline 87 \end{array}
\qquad
\begin{array}{r} 20 \\ +40 \\ \hline 39 \end{array}
$$

$$
\begin{array}{r} 59 \\ -37 \\ \hline 31 \end{array}
\qquad
\begin{array}{r} 43 \\ +22 \\ \hline 65 \end{array}
\qquad
\begin{array}{r} 15 \\ +14 \\ \hline 29 \end{array}
\qquad
\begin{array}{r} 99 \\ -33 \\ \hline 66 \end{array}
$$

Mystery Insect

▶ Find the answers.
Use the code to name the insect.

a = 24	b = 35	d = 22	g = 99
l = 16	u = 86	y = 17	

$$
\begin{array}{ccccccc}
99 & 87 & 59 & 78 & 69 & 42 & 54 \\
-83 & -63 & -37 & -61 & -34 & +44 & +45 \\
\hline
\boxed{16} & \square & \square & \square & \square & \square & \square \\
\end{array}
$$

l   __   __   __   __   __   __

▶ Draw the mystery insect.

Look at the graph to see the bugs I found.
Use the graph to answer the questions.

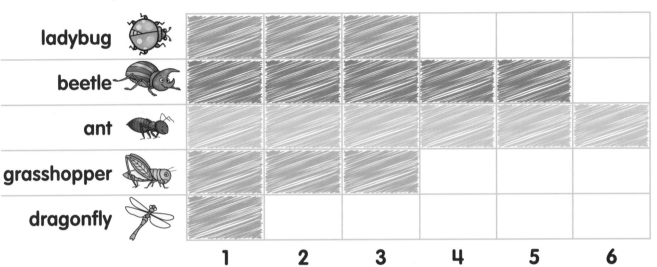

	1	2	3	4	5	6

1. How many more ants than dragonflies did I find?
   Show the number sentence.

   $$6 - 1 = 5$$

2. How many beetles and ants did I find?
   Show the number sentence.

   $$\square + \square = \square$$

3. How many more beetles than ladybugs did I find?
   Show the number sentence.

   $$\square - \square = \square$$

4. How many ants, ladybugs, and grasshoppers did I find?
   Show the number sentence.

   $$\square + \square + \square = \square$$

▶ Follow the path. Write the missing numbers from **1** to **50** to put the teddy bear in the toy box.

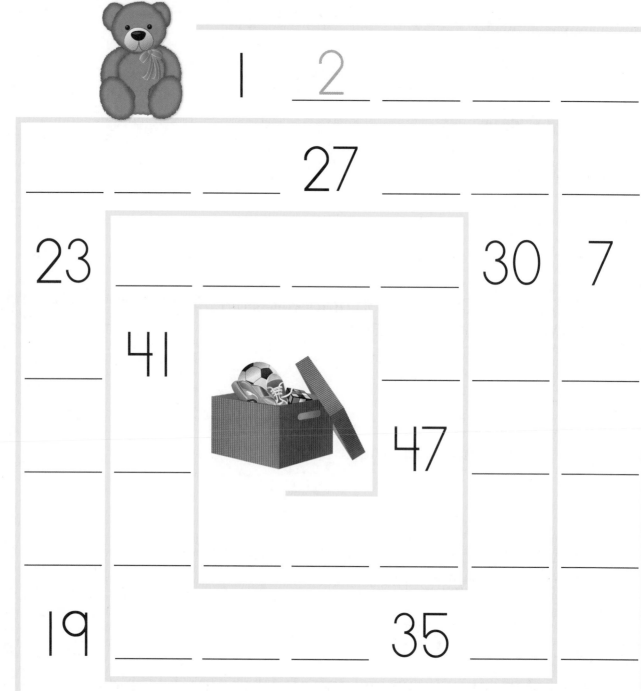

1   2   ___   ___   ___

___   ___   ___   27   ___

23   ___   ___   ___   ___   30   7

___   41

___

___   47

___

19   ___   ___   ___   35   ___

___   ___   ___   ___   12

EMC 4175 • © Evan-Moor Corp.

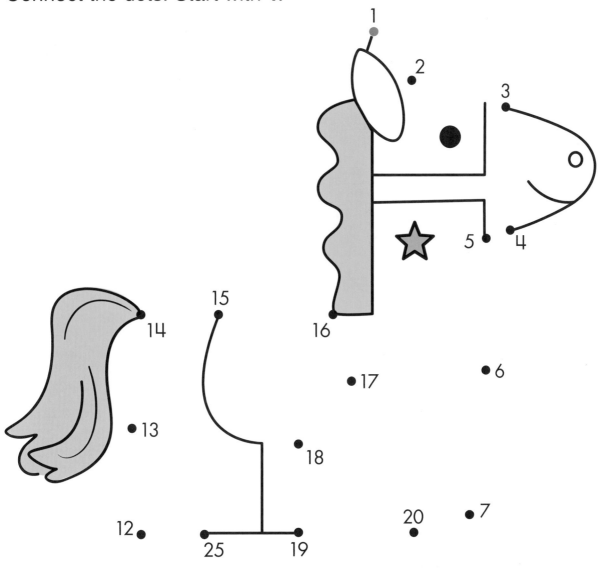

Connect the dots. Start with **1**.

More, Less, and In Between

▶ Write the missing numbers. Use the number chart.

1	2	3	4	5	6	7	8	9	10
11	12	13	14	15	16	17	18	19	20
21	22	23	24	25	26	27	28	29	30
31	32	33	34	35	36	37	38	39	40
41	42	43	44	45	46	47	48	49	50

one more

8 __9__

18 ____

16 ____

39 ____

47 ____

one less

__9__ 10

____ 30

____ 46

____ 50

____ 22

in between

1 __2__ 3

11 ____ 13

19 ____ 21

48 ____ 50

32 ____ 34

EMC 4175 • © Evan-Moor Corp.

13 is **less** than 15

13 $<$ 15

80 is **more** than 50

80 $>$ 50

▶ Write **<** or **>**.

19 $<$ 50   15 ◯ 50   51 ◯ 50

64 ◯ 50   49 ◯ 50   65 ◯ 50

83 ◯ 50   27 ◯ 50   33 ◯ 50

▶ Color the balls.
Red = numbers less than 50
Green = numbers more than 50

19   51   35

83   49   64

Add and Subtract to 5

▶ Find the answers.

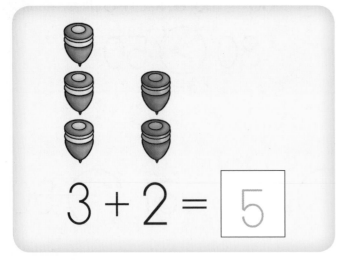

$3 + 2 = \boxed{5}$

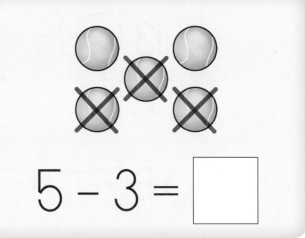

$5 - 3 = \boxed{}$

$2 + 1 = \boxed{}$

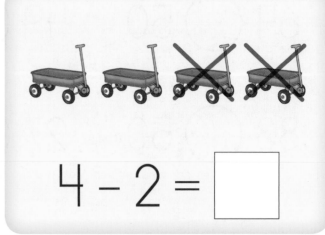

$4 - 2 = \boxed{}$

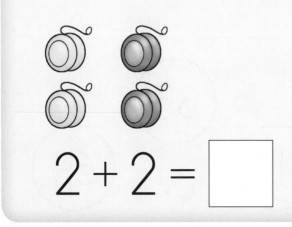

$2 + 2 = \boxed{}$

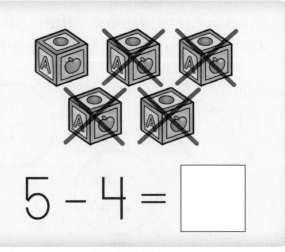

$5 - 4 = \boxed{}$

EMC 4175 • © Evan-Moor Corp.

Find the answers.

$$\begin{array}{r} 1 \\ +1 \\ \hline \boxed{2} \end{array} \qquad \begin{array}{r} 2 \\ +2 \\ \hline \boxed{} \end{array} \qquad \begin{array}{r} 4 \\ -0 \\ \hline \boxed{} \end{array} \qquad \begin{array}{r} 3 \\ -2 \\ \hline \boxed{} \end{array} \qquad \begin{array}{r} 5 \\ -5 \\ \hline \boxed{} \end{array}$$

$$\begin{array}{r} 5 \\ -4 \\ \hline \boxed{} \end{array} \qquad \begin{array}{r} 2 \\ +3 \\ \hline \boxed{} \end{array} \qquad \begin{array}{r} 5 \\ +0 \\ \hline \boxed{} \end{array} \qquad \begin{array}{r} 3 \\ -1 \\ \hline \boxed{} \end{array} \qquad \begin{array}{r} 1 \\ +2 \\ \hline \boxed{} \end{array}$$

$$\begin{array}{r} 2 \\ +0 \\ \hline \boxed{} \end{array} \qquad \begin{array}{r} 4 \\ -2 \\ \hline \boxed{} \end{array} \qquad \begin{array}{r} 3 \\ +1 \\ \hline \boxed{} \end{array} \qquad \begin{array}{r} 2 \\ -2 \\ \hline \boxed{} \end{array} \qquad \begin{array}{r} 2 \\ -1 \\ \hline \boxed{} \end{array}$$

Add and Subtract to 6

▶ Find the answers.

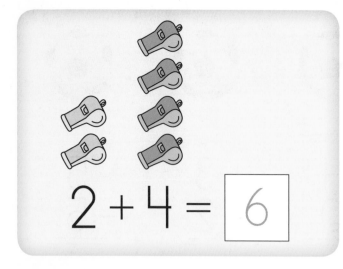

$2 + 4 = \boxed{6}$

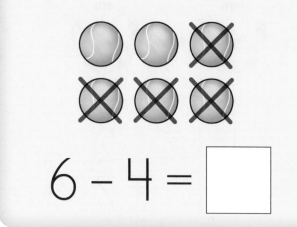

$6 - 4 = \boxed{}$

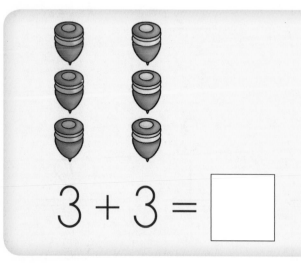

$3 + 3 = \boxed{}$

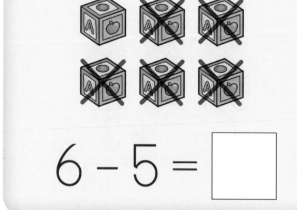

$6 - 5 = \boxed{}$

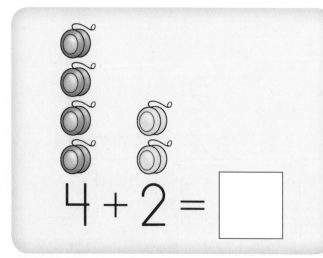

$4 + 2 = \boxed{}$

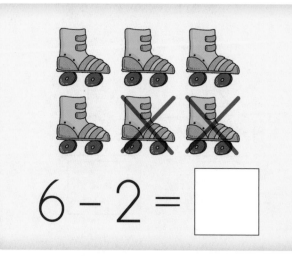

$6 - 2 = \boxed{}$

EMC 4175 • © Evan-Moor Corp.

▶ Find the answers.

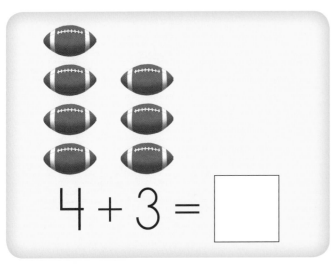

$5 + 5 = \boxed{10}$

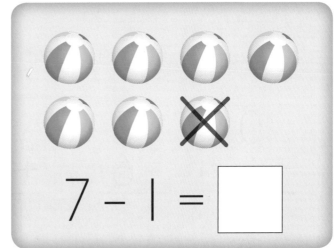

$7 - 5 = \boxed{}$

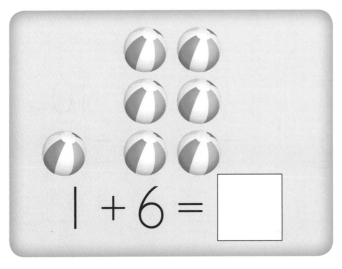

$4 + 3 = \boxed{}$

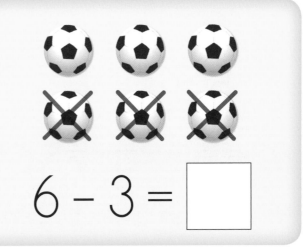

$7 - 1 = \boxed{}$

$1 + 6 = \boxed{}$

$6 - 3 = \boxed{}$

Add and Subtract to 10

▶ Find the answers.

$$\begin{array}{r} 1 \\ +5 \\ \hline \boxed{6} \end{array}$$
$$\begin{array}{r} 7 \\ -0 \\ \hline \boxed{} \end{array}$$
$$\begin{array}{r} 6 \\ -1 \\ \hline \boxed{} \end{array}$$
$$\begin{array}{r} 3 \\ +4 \\ \hline \boxed{} \end{array}$$
$$\begin{array}{r} 6 \\ +1 \\ \hline \boxed{} \end{array}$$

$$\begin{array}{r} 0 \\ +6 \\ \hline \boxed{} \end{array}$$
$$\begin{array}{r} 7 \\ -6 \\ \hline \boxed{} \end{array}$$
$$\begin{array}{r} 5 \\ +2 \\ \hline \boxed{} \end{array}$$
$$\begin{array}{r} 8 \\ -5 \\ \hline \boxed{} \end{array}$$
$$\begin{array}{r} 5 \\ +5 \\ \hline \boxed{} \end{array}$$

$$\begin{array}{r} 5 \\ -2 \\ \hline \boxed{} \end{array}$$
$$\begin{array}{r} 4 \\ -4 \\ \hline \boxed{} \end{array}$$
$$\begin{array}{r} 7 \\ +3 \\ \hline \boxed{} \end{array}$$
$$\begin{array}{r} 5 \\ -1 \\ \hline \boxed{} \end{array}$$
$$\begin{array}{r} 10 \\ -5 \\ \hline \boxed{} \end{array}$$

EMC 4175 • © Evan-Moor Corp.

▶ Make 2 addition and 2 subtraction problems.

1   2   3

| 1 + 2 = 3 |
| ___ + ___ = ___ |
| ___ − ___ = ___ |
| ___ − ___ = ___ |

6   3   9

| ___ + ___ = ___ |
| ___ + ___ = ___ |
| ___ − ___ = ___ |
| ___ − ___ = ___ |

2   5   7

| ___ + ___ = ___ |
| ___ + ___ = ___ |
| ___ − ___ = ___ |
| ___ − ___ = ___ |

5   9   4

| ___ + ___ = ___ |
| ___ + ___ = ___ |
| ___ − ___ = ___ |
| ___ − ___ = ___ |

Fact Families

Make 2 addition and 2 subtraction problems.

2 4 6

2 + 4 = 6

___ + ___ = ___

___ − ___ = ___

___ − ___ = ___

5 1 4

___ + ___ = ___

___ + ___ = ___

___ − ___ = ___

___ − ___ = ___

3 8 5

___ + ___ = ___

___ + ___ = ___

___ − ___ = ___

___ − ___ = ___

4 6 2

___ + ___ = ___

___ + ___ = ___

___ − ___ = ___

___ − ___ = ___

▶ Add.

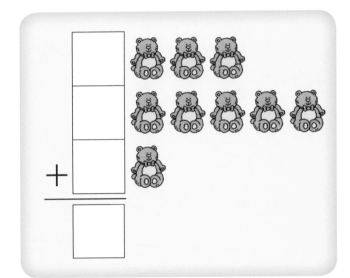

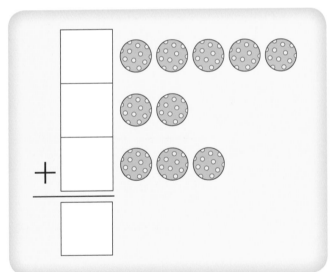

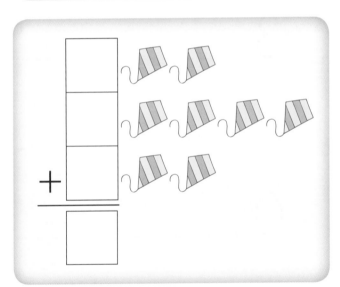

$$\begin{array}{r} 4 \\ 3 \\ +\ 1 \\ \hline 8 \end{array}$$

$$\begin{array}{r} 8 \\ 0 \\ +\ 2 \\ \hline \ \end{array}$$

$$\begin{array}{r} 6 \\ 1 \\ +\ 2 \\ \hline \ \end{array}$$

$$\begin{array}{r} 2 \\ 5 \\ +\ 2 \\ \hline \ \end{array}$$

$$\begin{array}{r} 3 \\ 4 \\ +\ 3 \\ \hline \ \end{array}$$

Name the Number

Write each number word.

0	1	2	3	4	5
zero	one	two	three	four	five
6	7	8	9	10	
six	seven	eight	nine	ten	

3 _three_

4 _____

10 _____

8 _____

0 _____

1 _____

7 _____

6 _____

2 _____

5 _____

9 _____

▶ Match the number with its name.

five

one

two

eight

four

nine

0
1
2
3
4
5
6
7
8
9
10

six

three

seven

zero

ten

Count by Tens

▶ Count by **10**s to **100**.

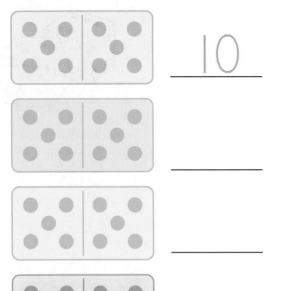 10

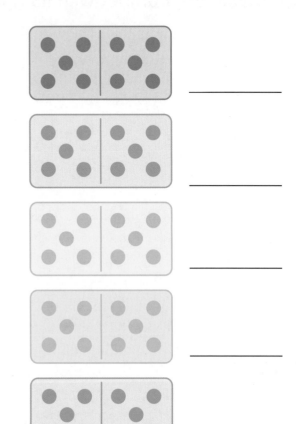 _____

_____

_____

_____

_____

_____

_____

_____

_____

▶ Connect the dots.
Count by **10**s.
Start with **10**.

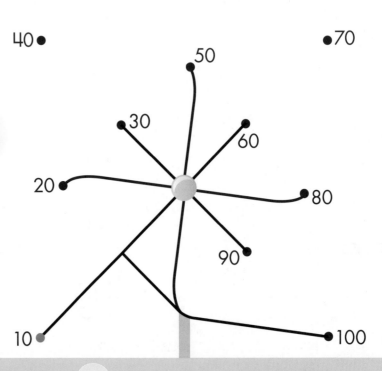

EMC 4175 • © Evan-Moor Corp.

▶ Count by **5**s to **50**.

▶ Connect the dots.
Count by **5**s.
Start with **5**.

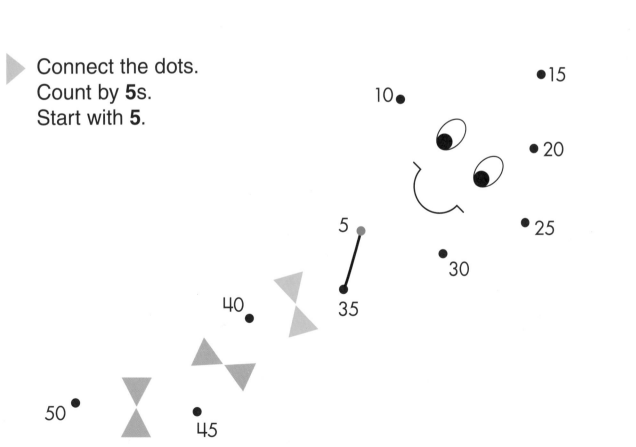

Count by Twos

▶ Count by **2**s to **20**.

_____   _____   _____   _____   _____

_____   _____   _____   _____   _____

▶ Connect the dots.
Count by **2**s.
Start with **2**.

▶ What comes next? Color it. Name it.

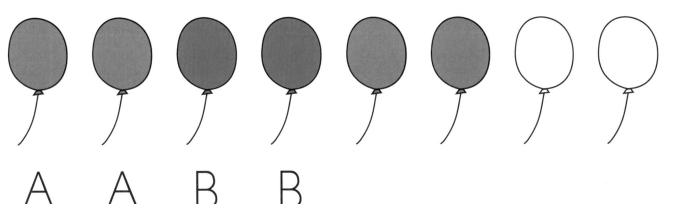

A   A   B   B   ___ ___ ___ ___

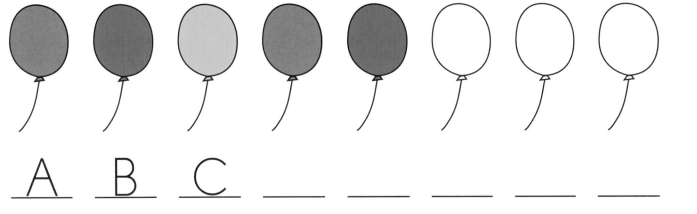

A   B   C   ___ ___ ___ ___ ___

___ ___ ___ ___ ___ ___ ___ ___

Patterns

▶ What shape comes next? Draw it.

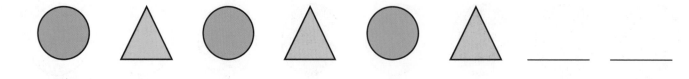

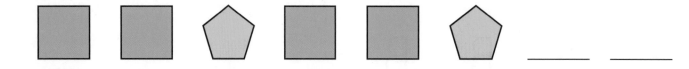

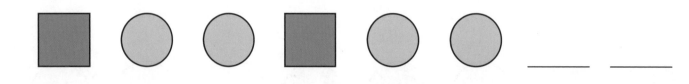

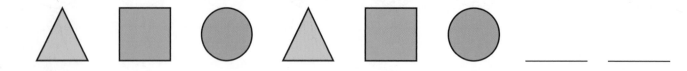

▶ What number comes next? Write it.

5 10 15 ___ ___ ___ ___

2 4 6 ___ ___ ___ ___

10 20 30 ___ ___ ___ ___

Color the numbers in order to get the toy race car to the finish line.
Count by **10**s. Start with **10**.

		10	50	30
40	30	20	70	40
50	100	60	10	20
60	70	80	90	60
10	50	20	100	70

FINISH

Count by Fives

Write the numbers in order from **5** to **50**
to get the baseball in the glove. Count by **5**s.

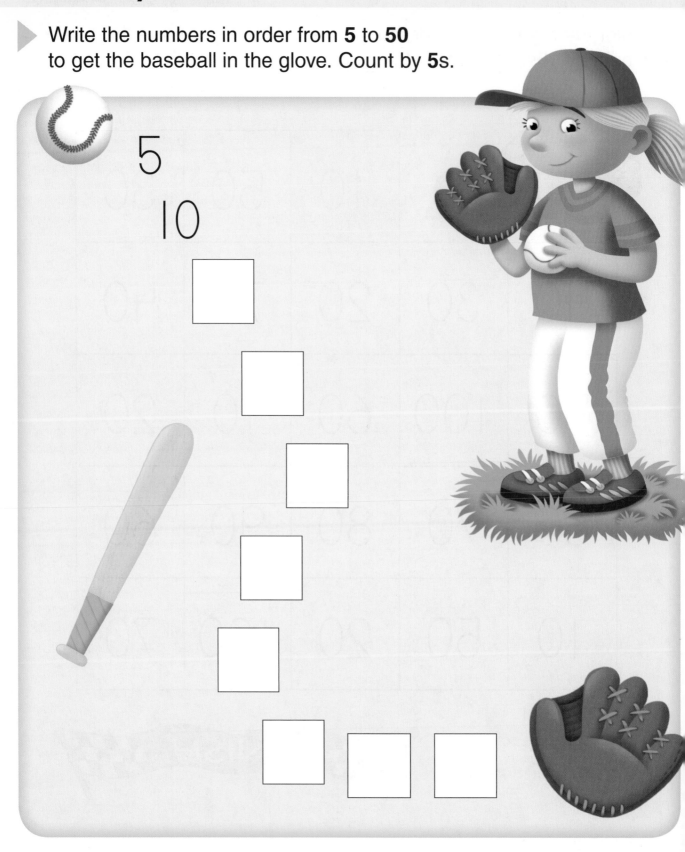

5

10

EMC 4175 • © Evan-Moor Corp.

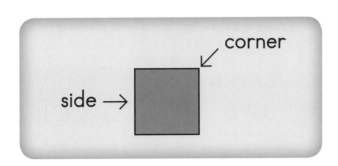

▶ Count the number of sides and corners.

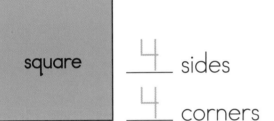

__4__ sides

__4__ corners

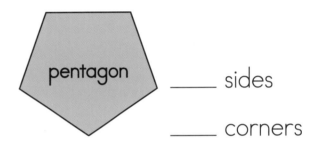

_____ sides

_____ corners

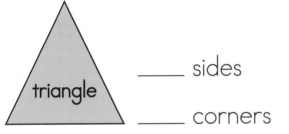

_____ sides

_____ corners

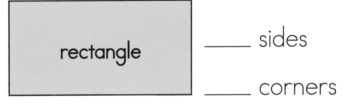

_____ sides

_____ corners

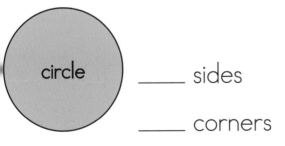

_____ sides

_____ corners

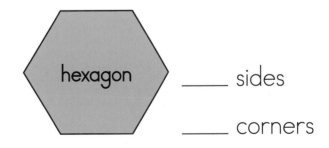

_____ sides

_____ corners

Shapes

▶ Draw a line to match the shape with its name.

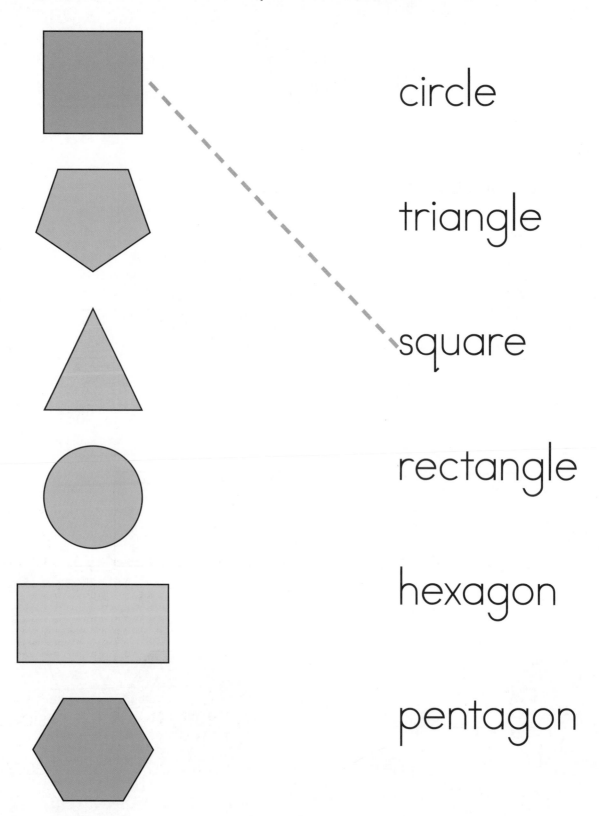

circle

triangle

square

rectangle

hexagon

pentagon

Read the shape names.
Color the toys.

triangle = pink

square = brown

rectangle = blue

circle = green

hexagon = red

pentagon = yellow

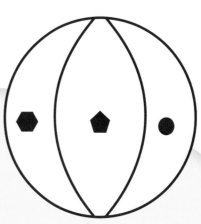

Count the Balls

▶ A box holds 10 balls. Circle groups of 10 balls for each box. Count how many balls are left.

How many boxes do you need? __1__

How many balls are left? __4__

How many boxes do you need? _____

How many balls are left? _____

How many boxes do you need? _____

How many balls are left? _____

EMC 4175 • © Evan-Moor Corp.

| ten = | | one = □ |

▶ Count the blocks to find the answers.

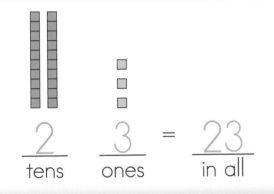

$$\underline{2} \quad \underline{3} \quad = \quad \underline{23}$$
tens   ones   in all

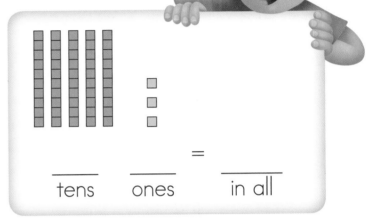

_____   _____   =   _____

tens   ones   in all

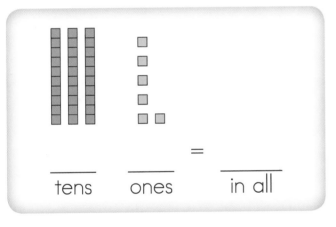

_____   _____   =   _____

tens   ones   in all

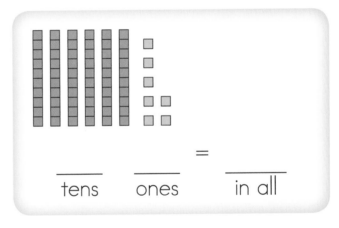

_____   _____   =   _____

tens   ones   in all

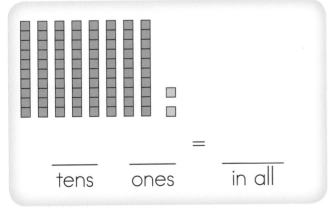

_____   _____   =   _____

tens   ones   in all

_____   _____   =   _____

tens   ones   in all

Dimes and Pennies

I ten =   I one =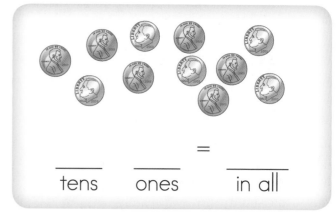

▶ Count the tens and ones. Write how many cents in all.

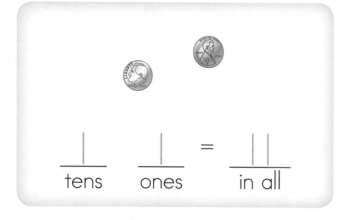

| _____ | _____ | = | _____ |
| tens | ones | | in all |

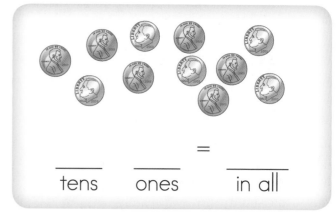

| _____ | _____ | = | _____ |
| tens | ones | | in all |

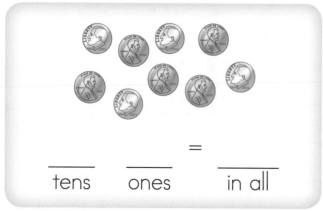

| _____ | _____ | = | _____ |
| tens | ones | | in all |

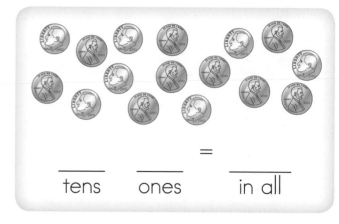

| _____ | _____ | = | _____ |
| tens | ones | | in all |

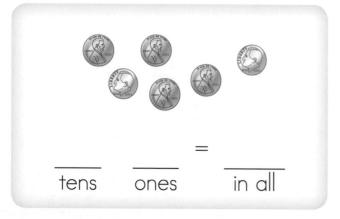

| _____ | _____ | = | _____ |
| tens | ones | | in all |

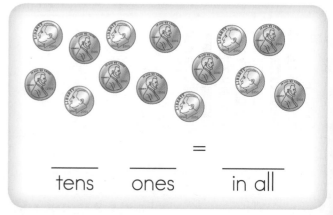

| _____ | _____ | = | _____ |
| tens | ones | | in all |

EMC 4175 • © Evan-Moor Corp.

What Time Is It?

Draw a line to match the clock to the time.

2:00

8:30

12:00

10:30

3:30

5:00

1:30

6:00

Balls for Sale

▶ Read the graph to see how many balls were sold.

	1	2	3	4	5	6
baseball						
soccer ball						
football						
tennis ball						

▶ How many?

 _____    _____    _____    _____

▶ Which sold the most? _____

▶ Which sold the least? _____

Answer Key

Please take time to go over the work your child has completed. Ask your child to explain what he or she has done. Praise both success and effort. If mistakes have been made, explain what the answer should have been and how to find it. Let your child know that mistakes are a part of learning. The time you spend with your child helps let him or her know you feel learning is important.

Page 2
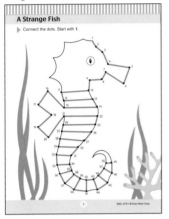

Page 3
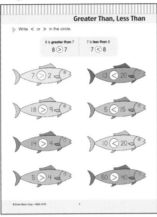

Page 4
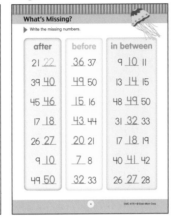

Page 5
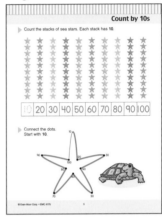

Page 6
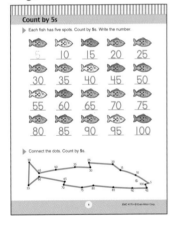

Page 7

Page 8
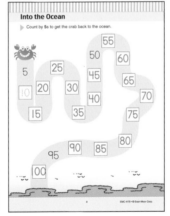

Page 9

Page 10

Page 11
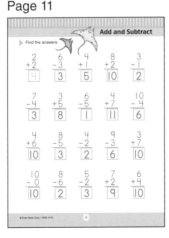

Page 12
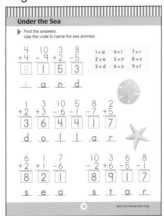

Page 13

Page 14

Word Search

Find the hidden numbers. Circle them.

zero three six nine twelve
one   four   seven ten two
five eight eleven

n o n e s i x g d w
o h z e r o o f i c
h e i g h t u x r p
t h r e e v s m o n
t e n t w e l v e g
f o u r s e v e n g
n i n e g d d s m l
t w o y c f i v e x
e l e v e n n v s k

Page 15

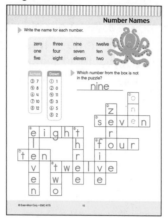

Number Names

Write the name for each number.

zero three nine twelve
one   four   seven ten
five eight eleven two

Across / Down

Which number from the box is not in the puzzle? **nine**

(crossword with: zero, seven, on, eight, three, four, ten, twelve, two)

Page 16

Crab Maze

Find the answers. Help the mama crab get to her baby crabs. Color boxes with the answer 9 blue.

$7+2=9$ $8+4=12$ $9+5=14$ $10+5=15$ $14-9=5$

$12-6=6$ $13-3=10$ ...

Page 17

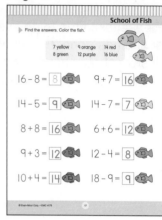

School of Fish

Find the answers. Color the fish.

7 yellow 9 orange 14 red
8 green   12 purple 16 blue

$16-8=8$ $9+7=16$
$14-5=9$ $14-7=7$
$8+8=16$ $6+6=12$
$9+3=12$ $12-4=8$
$10+4=14$ $18-9=9$

Page 18

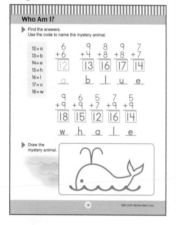

Who Am I?

Find the answers. Use the code to name the mystery animal.

12=a 13=b 14=e 15=h 16=i 17=u 18=w

$6+6=12$ $9+4=13$ $8+8=16$ $9+8=17$ $7+7=14$

_a_ _b_ _l_ _u_ _e_

$9+9=18$ $6+9=15$ $5+7=12$ $7+7=14$ $9+5=14$

_w_ _h_ _a_ _l_ _e_

Draw the mystery animal.

Page 19

Fact Families

Fact families have 2 addition sentences and 2 subtraction sentences made from 3 numbers. Complete each fact family.

2 8 10
$2+8=10$
$8+2=10$
$10-2=8$
$10-8=2$

9 5 14
$9+5=14$
$5+9=14$
$14-9=5$
$14-5=9$

6 7 13
$6+7=13$
$7+6=13$
$13-7=6$
$13-6=7$

8 4 12
$8+4=12$
$4+8=12$
$12-8=4$
$12-4=8$

Page 20

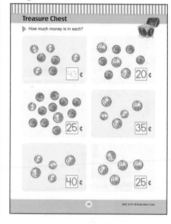

Treasure Chest

How much money is in each?

43¢   20¢
25¢   35¢
40¢   25¢

Page 21

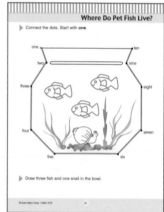

Where Do Pet Fish Live?

Connect the dots. Start with one.

one two three four five six seven eight nine ten

Draw three fish and one snail in the bowl.

Page 22

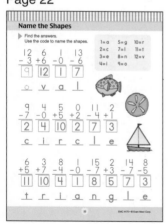

Name the Shapes

Find the answers. Use the code to name the shapes.

1=a 5=g 10=r
2=c 7=l 11=t
3=e 8=n 12=v
4=i 9=o

$12-3=9$ $6+6=12$ $1-0=1$ $13-6=7$

_o_ _v_ _a_ _l_

$9-7=2$ $4-0=4$ $5+5=10$ $0+2=2$ $11+2=13$

_c_ _i_ _r_ _c_ _l_ _e_

$6+5=11$ $3+7=10$ $8-4=4$ $1-0=1$ $15-7=8$ $2+3=5$ $14-7=7$ $8-5=3$

_t_ _r_ _i_ _a_ _n_ _g_ _l_ _e_

Page 23

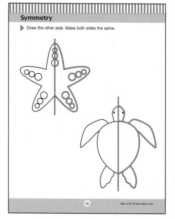

Word Search

Find the hidden shape names. Circle them.

○ circle   □ rectangle   ☆ star
□ square   ⬠ pentagon   ♥ heart
△ triangle ○ oval   ○ hexagon

s x c i r c l e t o s
t r p e n t a g o n q
a m c t h e a r t c u
r o m h e x a g o n a
o v a l c h n i r z r
n b t r i a n g l e e
r e c t a n g l e s e

Page 24

Symmetry

Draw the other side. Make both sides the same.

Page 25

Gone Fishing

The children went fishing on Saturday. Use the graph to answer the questions.

Bob	🐟🐟🐟🐟🐟
Kim	🐟🐟🐟🐟
Raul	🐟🐟🐟🐟🐟🐟🐟
Kai	🐟🐟🐟
Max	🐟🐟🐟🐟🐟🐟

1. How many fish did each child catch?
Bob _5_ Kim _4_ Raul _7_
Kai _3_ Max _6_

2. Who caught the most? _Raul_

3. Who caught the fewest? _Kai_

4. How many more fish did Raul catch than Kai? _4_

Page 26

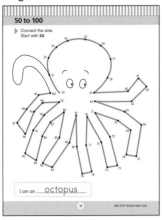

50 to 100
Connect the dots. Start with **50**.

I am an **octopus**

Page 27

Find the Octopus
Read and follow the directions.

1. Start at the
2. Go right **3** boxes. What do you see? **turtle**
3. Go down **2** boxes. What do you see? **crab**
4. Go right **3** boxes. What do you see? **fish**
5. Go up **4** boxes. What do you see? **octopus**

Page 28

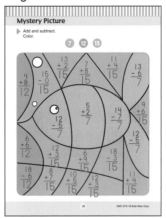

Mystery Picture
Add and subtract. Color.

Page 29

Count to 100
Write the numbers **1** to **100** in order.

1	2	3	4	5	6	7	8	9	10
11	12	13	14	15	16	17	18	19	20
21	22	23	24	25	26	27	28	29	30
31	32	33	34	35	36	37	38	39	40
41	42	43	44	45	46	47	48	49	50
51	52	53	54	55	56	57	58	59	60
61	62	63	64	65	66	67	68	69	70
71	72	73	74	75	76	77	78	79	80
81	82	83	84	85	86	87	88	89	90
91	92	93	94	95	96	97	98	99	100

Page 30

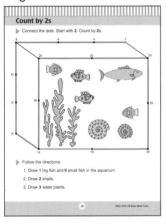

Count by 2s
Connect the dots. Start with **2**. Count by **2s**.

Follow the directions.
1. Draw **1** big fish and **4** small fish in the aquarium.
2. Draw **2** snails.
3. Draw **3** water plants.

Page 31

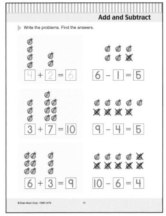

Add and Subtract
Write the problems. Find the answers.

$4 + 2 = 6$ $6 - 1 = 5$

$3 + 7 = 10$ $9 - 4 = 5$

$6 + 3 = 9$ $10 - 6 = 4$

Page 32

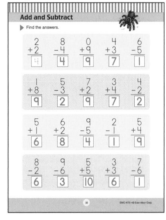

Add and Subtract
Find the answers.

$2 + 2 = 4$ $8 - 4 = 4$ $0 + 9 = 9$ $4 + 3 = 7$ $6 - 5 = 1$

$1 + 8 = 9$ $5 - 3 = 2$ $7 + 2 = 9$ $3 + 4 = 7$ $4 - 2 = 2$

$5 + 1 = 6$ $6 + 2 = 8$ $9 - 5 = 4$ $2 - 1 = 1$ $5 + 4 = 9$

$8 - 2 = 6$ $9 - 6 = 3$ $5 + 5 = 10$ $3 + 3 = 6$ $7 - 6 = 1$

Page 33

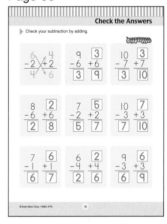

Check the Answers
Check your subtraction by adding.

Page 34

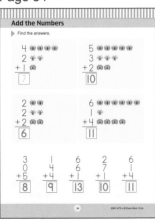

Add the Numbers
Find the answers.

$4 + 2 + 1 = 7$ $5 + 3 + 2 = 10$

$2 + 2 + 2 = 6$ $6 + 1 + 4 = 11$

$3 + 0 + 5 = 8$ $1 + 4 + 4 = 9$ $6 + 6 + 1 = 13$ $2 + 7 + 1 = 10$ $6 + 1 + 4 = 11$

Page 35

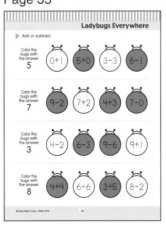

Ladybugs Everywhere
Add or subtract.

Color the bugs with the answer **5**
$0+1$ $5+0$ $3-3$ $6-1$

Color the bugs with the answer **7**
$9-2$ $7+2$ $4+3$ $7-0$

Color the bugs with the answer **3**
$4-2$ $6-3$ $9-6$ $9+1$

Color the bugs with the answer **8**
$4+4$ $6-6$ $3+5$ $8-2$

Page 36

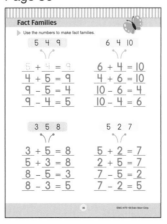

Fact Families
Use the numbers to make fact families.

5 4 9
$5 + 4 = 9$
$4 + 5 = 9$
$9 - 5 = 4$
$9 - 4 = 5$

6 4 10
$6 + 4 = 10$
$4 + 6 = 10$
$10 - 6 = 4$
$10 - 4 = 6$

3 5 8
$3 + 5 = 8$
$5 + 3 = 8$
$8 - 5 = 3$
$8 - 3 = 5$

5 2 7
$5 + 2 = 7$
$2 + 5 = 7$
$7 - 5 = 2$
$7 - 2 = 5$

Page 37

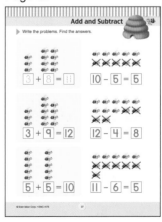

Add and Subtract
Write the problems. Find the answers.

$3 + 8 = 11$ $10 - 5 = 5$

$3 + 9 = 12$ $12 - 4 = 8$

$5 + 5 = 10$ $11 - 6 = 5$

Page 38

Page 39

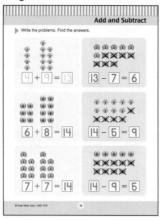

Page 40

Page 41

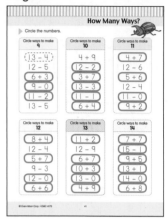

Page 42

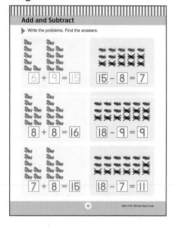

Page 43

Page 44

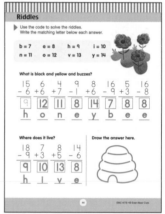

Page 45

Page 46

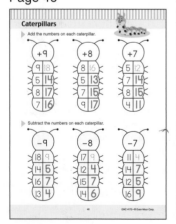

Page 47

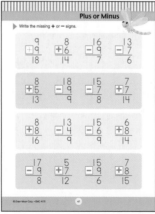

Page 48

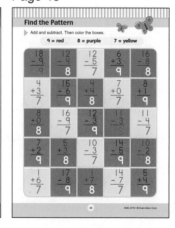

Page 49

EMC 4175 • © Evan-Moor Corp.

Page 50

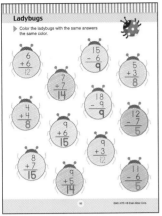

Ladybugs

Page 51

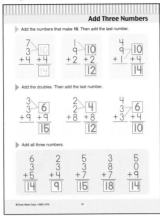

Add Three Numbers

Page 52

Fact Families

Page 53

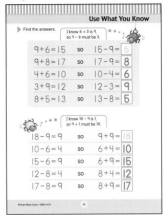

Use What You Know

Page 54

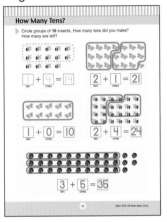

How Many Tens?

Page 55

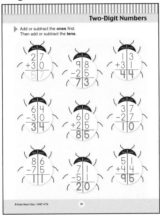

Two-Digit Numbers

Page 56

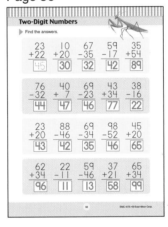

Two-Digit Numbers

Page 57

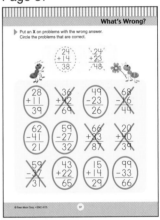

What's Wrong?

Page 58

Mystery Insect

Page 59

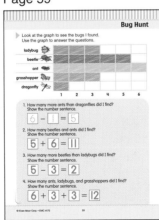

Bug Hunt

Page 60

Count to 50

Page 61

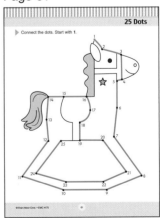

25 Dots

Page 62

More, Less, and In Between

Write the missing numbers. Use the number chart.

one more	one less	in between
8 _9_	_9_ 10	1 _2_ 3
18 _19_	_29_ 30	11 _12_ 13
16 _17_	_45_ 46	19 _20_ 21
39 _40_	_49_ 50	48 _49_ 50
47 _48_	_21_ 22	32 _33_ 34

Page 63

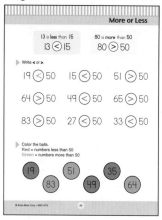

More or Less

13 is less than 15
13 $<$ 15

80 is more than 50
80 $>$ 50

Write < or >.

19 $<$ 50   15 $<$ 50   51 $>$ 50

64 $>$ 50   49 $<$ 50   65 $>$ 50

83 $>$ 50   27 $<$ 50   33 $<$ 50

Color the balls.
Red = numbers less than 50
Green = numbers more than 50

19   51   35
83   49   64

Page 64

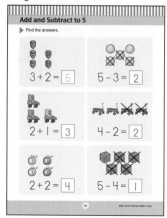

Add and Subtract to 5

Find the answers.

$3 + 2 =$ 5 $5 - 3 =$ 2

$2 + 1 =$ 3 $4 - 2 =$ 2

$2 + 2 =$ 4 $5 - 4 =$ 1

Page 65

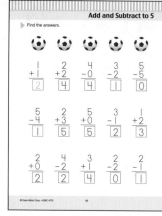

Add and Subtract to 5

Find the answers.

$\begin{array}{r} 1 \\ +1 \\ \hline 2 \end{array}$ $\begin{array}{r} 2 \\ +2 \\ \hline 4 \end{array}$ $\begin{array}{r} 4 \\ -0 \\ \hline 4 \end{array}$ $\begin{array}{r} 3 \\ -2 \\ \hline 1 \end{array}$ $\begin{array}{r} 5 \\ -5 \\ \hline 0 \end{array}$

$\begin{array}{r} 5 \\ -4 \\ \hline 1 \end{array}$ $\begin{array}{r} 2 \\ +3 \\ \hline 5 \end{array}$ $\begin{array}{r} 5 \\ +0 \\ \hline 5 \end{array}$ $\begin{array}{r} 3 \\ -1 \\ \hline 2 \end{array}$ $\begin{array}{r} 1 \\ +2 \\ \hline 3 \end{array}$

$\begin{array}{r} 2 \\ +0 \\ \hline 2 \end{array}$ $\begin{array}{r} 4 \\ -2 \\ \hline 2 \end{array}$ $\begin{array}{r} 3 \\ +1 \\ \hline 4 \end{array}$ $\begin{array}{r} 2 \\ -2 \\ \hline 0 \end{array}$ $\begin{array}{r} 2 \\ -1 \\ \hline 1 \end{array}$

Page 66

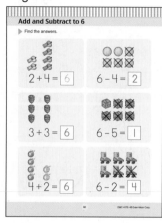

Add and Subtract to 6

Find the answers.

$2 + 4 =$ 6 $6 - 4 =$ 2

$3 + 3 =$ 6 $6 - 5 =$ 1

$4 + 2 =$ 6 $6 - 2 =$ 4

Page 67

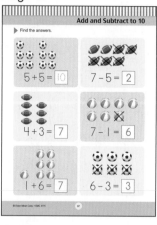

Add and Subtract to 10

Find the answers.

$5 + 5 =$ 10 $7 - 5 =$ 2

$4 + 3 =$ 7 $7 - 1 =$ 6

$1 + 6 =$ 7 $6 - 3 =$ 3

Page 68

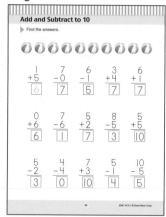

Add and Subtract to 10

Find the answers.

$\begin{array}{r} 1 \\ +5 \\ \hline 6 \end{array}$ $\begin{array}{r} 7 \\ -0 \\ \hline 7 \end{array}$ $\begin{array}{r} 6 \\ -1 \\ \hline 5 \end{array}$ $\begin{array}{r} 3 \\ +4 \\ \hline 7 \end{array}$ $\begin{array}{r} 6 \\ +1 \\ \hline 7 \end{array}$

$\begin{array}{r} 0 \\ +6 \\ \hline 6 \end{array}$ $\begin{array}{r} 7 \\ -6 \\ \hline 1 \end{array}$ $\begin{array}{r} 5 \\ +2 \\ \hline 7 \end{array}$ $\begin{array}{r} 8 \\ -5 \\ \hline 3 \end{array}$ $\begin{array}{r} 5 \\ +5 \\ \hline 10 \end{array}$

$\begin{array}{r} 5 \\ -2 \\ \hline 3 \end{array}$ $\begin{array}{r} 4 \\ -4 \\ \hline 0 \end{array}$ $\begin{array}{r} 7 \\ +3 \\ \hline 10 \end{array}$ $\begin{array}{r} 5 \\ -1 \\ \hline 4 \end{array}$ $\begin{array}{r} 10 \\ -5 \\ \hline 5 \end{array}$

Page 69

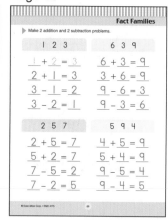

Fact Families

Make 2 addition and 2 subtraction problems.

1 2 3	6 3 9
$1 + 2 = 3$	$6 + 3 = 9$
$2 + 1 = 3$	$3 + 6 = 9$
$3 - 1 = 2$	$9 - 6 = 3$
$3 - 2 = 1$	$9 - 3 = 6$

2 5 7	5 9 4
$2 + 5 = 7$	$4 + 5 = 9$
$5 + 2 = 7$	$5 + 4 = 9$
$7 - 5 = 2$	$9 - 5 = 4$
$7 - 2 = 5$	$9 - 4 = 5$

Page 70

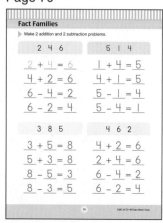

Fact Families

Make 2 addition and 2 subtraction problems.

2 4 6	5 1 4
$2 + 4 = 6$	$1 + 4 = 5$
$4 + 2 = 6$	$4 + 1 = 5$
$6 - 4 = 2$	$5 - 1 = 4$
$6 - 2 = 4$	$5 - 4 = 1$

3 8 5	4 6 2
$3 + 5 = 8$	$4 + 2 = 6$
$5 + 3 = 8$	$2 + 4 = 6$
$8 - 5 = 3$	$6 - 4 = 2$
$8 - 3 = 5$	$6 - 2 = 4$

Page 71

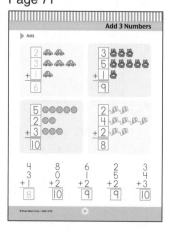

Add 3 Numbers

Add.

$\begin{array}{r} 2 \\ 3 \\ +1 \\ \hline 6 \end{array}$ $\begin{array}{r} 3 \\ 5 \\ +1 \\ \hline 9 \end{array}$

$\begin{array}{r} 5 \\ 2 \\ +3 \\ \hline 10 \end{array}$ $\begin{array}{r} 2 \\ 4 \\ +2 \\ \hline 8 \end{array}$

$\begin{array}{r} 4 \\ 3 \\ +1 \\ \hline 8 \end{array}$ $\begin{array}{r} 8 \\ 0 \\ +2 \\ \hline 10 \end{array}$ $\begin{array}{r} 6 \\ 1 \\ +2 \\ \hline 9 \end{array}$ $\begin{array}{r} 2 \\ 5 \\ +2 \\ \hline 9 \end{array}$ $\begin{array}{r} 3 \\ 4 \\ +3 \\ \hline 10 \end{array}$

Page 72

Name the Number

Write each number word.

0	1	2	3	4	5
zero	one	two	three	four	five

6	7	8	9	10
six	seven	eight	nine	ten

3 _three_   4 _four_

10 _ten_   8 _eight_

0 _zero_   1 _one_

7 _seven_   6 _six_

2 _two_   5 _five_

9 _nine_

Page 73

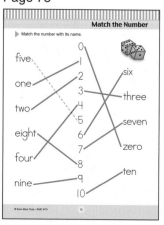

Match the Number

Match the number with its name.

five — 0
one — 1
two — 2
eight — 3 — three
four — 4
nine — 5 — seven
— 6
— 7 — zero
— 8
— 9 — ten
— 10 — six

EMC 4175 • © Evan-Moor Corp.

Page 74
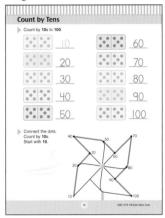

Page 75
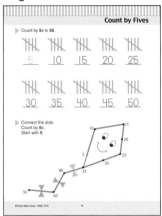

Page 76
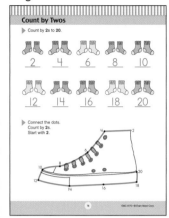

Page 77
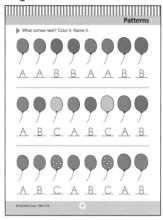

Page 78
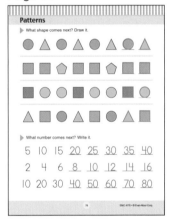

Page 79
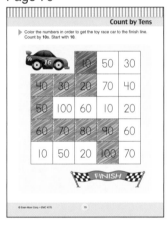

Page 80
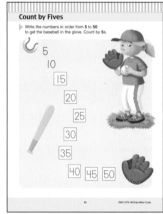

Page 81
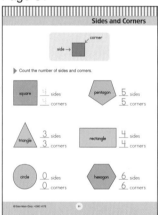

Page 82
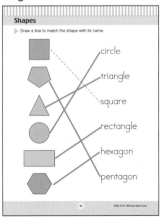

Page 83

Page 84
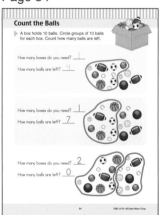

Page 85
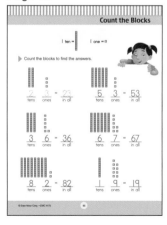

Page 86

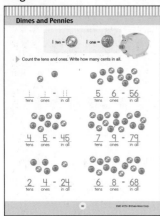

Page 87

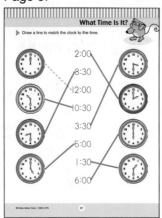

Page 88

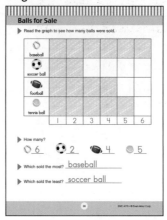